THE GOLDAPPLE GUIDE TO

JEWISH BERLIN

ANDREW ROTH

and

MICHAEL FRAJMAN

Goldapple
Publishing

The authors would like to thank the following people for their help and advice: Peter Ambros, Jaques Bagios, Kevin Cote, Jack Holland, Nicola Galliner, Jerold James Gordon, Michael Jack, Sylvie Kajdi, Dorothee Kocevar, Suzanna Lauterbach, Carol Levy, Joel Levy, Stefan Liebig, Dirk Lindemann, Andreas Nachama, Sara Nachama, Rabbi Yehuda Teichtel, Ed Ward and Oliver Wilking. Thanks as well to the many others, unnamed here, who have contributed to this book.

Published by Goldapple Publishing
Eylauer Strasse 3
D-10965 Berlin, Germany
goldapple@compuserve.com

Design and production by Lindemann Bagios, Berlin, Germany
Printing by Wiener Verlag, Himberg, Austria

Cover Design by Jaques Bagios
Cover Collage Photos:
Moses Mendelssohn—Deutsches Historisches Museum Archive;
Cantor Estrongo Nachama and Bat Mitzvah—Suzanna
Lauterbach; Einstein marker—A. Only; Café Oren sign—A. Only;
New Synagogue—Berlin Tourismus Marketing

ISBN 3-9806356-0-0

To Ella Lillian and Tessa Helene, Berliners.

A.R.

To Sylvie.

M.F.

Highlights and Recommendations

Although Berlin never had a Jewish ghetto, a large number of interesting sites are concentrated in the Mitte district, the historic center of town. If your time is limited, a day spent here, in what is often, if not quite accurately called the Scheunenviertel (the Barn Quarter), can quickly deliver a sense of the Jewish past and present. The most important highlights in this neighborhood are the Centrum Judaicum-New Synagogue museum and cultural center, the site of the city's first Jewish Cemetery on Grosse Hamburger Strasse, the Jewish secondary school next door, the Adass Yisroel synagogue and offices, and the building of the former Hochschule für die Wissenschaft des Judentums (the College for the Science of Judaism). A two- to three-hour stroll to these and other sites can be found in the walking tour.

Among other notable sites you may want to visit are the Weisensee Cemetery, the Schönhauser Allee Cemetery, the Jewish Museum, The House of the Wannsee Conference Memorial Center, the Topography of Terror, and the Jewish Community Center.

For those looking for a "typical Berlin" Shabbat service, try the Pestalozzistrasse Synagogue, which features a traditional, German-style liberal liturgy. A lively and informal Kabbalat Shabbat service where visitors are welcome takes place at the Jewish Culture Society.

Foreword

This guidebook—long overdue—is the best indication that Jewish life in Berlin is once again a draw for tourists. I find it characteristic that it was an American in Berlin—a newcomer—who founded a publishing company to seize upon this opportunity.

For me personally it was the restoration of the cupola of the New Synagogue, the emblem of Jewish Berlin, that marked the "turning point" in the return of Berlin to the map of Jewish Europe. In 1989, a few months before the fall of the Berlin Wall, at a time when hardly anybody guessed that the days of the German Democratic Republic were numbered, construction work began on the former New Synagogue on Oranienburger Strasse, and directly thereafter the first English- and French-speaking tourists traveled to the what was then a truly gloomy area of East Berlin. One could tangibly sense that on this spot something of the former splendor of the synagogue, once one of Europe's most magnificent Jewish buildings, would again take shape.

Who would have thought that Jewish life in Berlin would take on completely new contours as a result of the opening of the east? At that time, there were about 6000 Jews in the city. Today there are at least twice as many. The majority of these newcomers are from the former Soviet Union. The growing attractiveness of Berlin, however, has also brought Jews from other western countries to our city, not least from Israel and the United States. A look at the Berlin Jewish Community today is a look at the whole world. Here one can find long-resident "Yekkes," children of middle- or eastern-European "displaced persons," Sephardic Jews, immigrants from the Commonwealth of Independent States and a growing "American-Jewish community." Under the symbolic roof of the *Einheitsgemeinde*—the single, state-sanctioned umbrella organization of Jews—all branches of Judaism, from ultra-orthodox to ultra-liberal, are gathered.

This positive development should not of course distract us from the fact that we live in a country that was not only responsible for the Shoah, but also in which xenophobia, racism and anti-Semitism capture headlines regularly. After the Second World War, the American military governor, General Clay, once said that German democracy would be measured by the way that the country treats its Jews. From the beginning, the Berlin Jewish Community has played a political role as a watchdog against any neo-Naziism—a role that is exercises with the same intensity today.

At the same time though, as the decades-long struggle over the Jewish Museum and its political-cultural autonomy shows, a new era in Jewish life has arrived; a life no longer based solely on remembrance of the Shoah and what preceded it. Therefore I wish to thank Goldapple Publishing for making this guidebook to Jewish Berlin possible, and above all its authors Andrew Roth and Michael Frajman, for realizing this courageous enterprise.

Dr. Andreas Nachama
Chairman of the Jewish Community of Berlin

Contents

Introduction

Berlin was once one of the great Jewish cities of the world. Like New York, London, Warsaw and Prague, it teemed with Jewish talent and industry. The importance of Berlin in modern Jewish history is hard to overestimate. Many of the issues that still animate and agitate Jews today—reform, assimilation, secularism, and modernity—first emerged in this city. It was here that Judaism first encountered and embraced the modern world, here that the early seeds of the reform and conservative movement were sown, here where modern Jewish historical scholarship was founded, and here where Jews plunged deeper and more successfully into mainstream cultural, commercial, political and scientific life than anywhere else on the continent.

Berlin's stature as a leading world capital—its rise in the nineteenth century to economic mastery and its renown in the early twentieth century for scientific accomplishment and artistic experimentation—was powered to a great extent by Jewish initiative.

The list of notables who once walked these streets is astonishing in its length and variety. It reaches back two hundred years to Moses Mendelssohn, who almost single-handedly brought the Enlightenment to Europe's Jews, and extends to such very diverse talents as Albert Einstein, Heinrich Heine, Rosa Luxemburg, Felix Mendelssohn, Marc Chagall, Karl Marx, Arnold Schoenberg, and Max Reinhardt.

A catalog of religious figures who once called Berlin home is no less impressive, including, among others, Martin Buber, Leo Baeck, Solomon Schechter, Menachem Schneerson, Abraham Joshua Heschel, and Joseph Ber Soloveichik.

That extraordinary and eminent society, of course, was obliterated, for it was here too, in the German capital, that the Nazi government was headquartered. Some 55,000 Berlin Jews were deported and murdered in the camps, another 80,000 were able to flee the Third Reich. The rich culture they created is no more.

Yet Jewish Berlin lives.

Reinvigorated by a huge influx of Jews from the former Soviet

Union, and energized by the vitality of a new generation, Jewish Berlin is larger and brasher than it has been in 50 years. The number of affiliated Jews in the city has almost doubled in the last decade to about 11,000, a lively array of grassroots groups and clubs have lately sprung up, and there is a prominent new public presence reflected in several Jewish and Israeli restaurants and cafés, kosher grocery stores, concerts and cultural events.

Today Jewish Berlin boasts seven synagogues, services from Reform to rigorously Orthodox, a school system that can take a child from kindergarten to high school, a youth center, an adult education program, several libraries, and enough concerts, lectures, films and parties to keep you away from home nearly every day of the week.

As before the Third Reich, Berlin has the largest number of Jews of any German city. As before, it has more synagogues than any other German city. As before, it is the headquarters to the major national Jewish organizations and home to many of the country's most prominent Jews. For a community that just ten or fifteen years ago seemed to be slowly fading out of existence, it is a remarkable recovery.

Not everyone thinks that this is necessarily a good thing. Many Jews feel that there is something wrong—something unbecoming, even slightly traitorous—about living in the land that gave birth to the Holocaust. Conversely, there are those who feel that a Germany free of Jews would be a posthumous victory for Hitler and that a Jewish presence here makes an important statement.

This debate, important as it is, lies beyond the scope of a travel guide. It is enough for our purposes that there is a renowned past worth exploring and a fascinating present worth experiencing. We hope that the *Goldapple Guide to Jewish Berlin* will help you to do both.

1 | Congregations & Synagogues

In contrast to the independent, synagogue-centered congregations of the United States and Great Britain, Berlin has a single, state-sanctioned entity, the *Jüdische Gemeinde zu Berlin*—the Jewish Community of Berlin—that functions as an umbrella organization for all the Jews in Berlin (with the exception of the small Adass Yisroel Orthodox congregation, which enjoys an independent legal status). This structure has been the norm in Germany since the inception of the modern Jewish community in the eighteenth century, and the Lutheran and Catholic churches are organized in much the same way. There is no separation of church and state in Germany.

With a single organization taking care of almost all needs and functions, Jewish life tends to be a little less intimate and a little more bureaucratized than is generally the case in the United States or Great Britain. On the other hand, this centralization makes possible an extraordinary array of activities and services.

■ Mikvot

There are two mikvot in Berlin, one located by the Orthodox synagogue at Joachimstaler Strasse 13 and another, recently built, at the New Synagogue at Oranienburger Strasse 28. Only one is in use however, and oddly enough it is the older mikveh on Joachimstaler Strasse, rather than the new facility. To arrange a visit, contact the Jewish Community organization's *Kultusabteilung* (Religious Affairs Department) at 880 28124.

CONGREGATIONS

Jüdische Gemeinde zu Berlin
(The Jewish Community of Berlin)

Fasanenstrasse 79–80 (administrative offices) (tel: 880 280). **Transportation:** *U-Bahn line U2 or U9 to Zoologischer Garten or U15 to Uhlandstrasse; S-Bahn line S3, S5, S7 or S9 to Zoologischer Garten; Bus 109, 119, 129 or 219 to Uhlandstrasse.* **Open:** *Monday–Thursday 9am–6pm, Friday until 3pm.*

The Jewish Community is the central organ of Jewish life in Berlin. It oversees all aspects of the synagogues, from cantor to cleaner.

The Community administers welfare and social services; runs schools, adult education classes, and outreach programs; and maintains two cemeteries, an old-age home, two libraries, and three administration centers. It publishes a monthly magazine, sponsors religious and social clubs, and organizes cultural events. The organization represents local Jewish interests and "the Jewish opinion" to the government and the media. Like the Lutheran and Catholic churches in Germany, it is empowered to collect taxes from members and receives government money for its activities.

Any Jew residing in Berlin is eligible for membership. Applicants must provide proof that they are Jewish (not always an easy task); non-Jewish family members are not accepted. There are at present about 11,000 members of the Jewish Community organization, and this figure is thus the official number of Jews in Berlin. However, this number actually represents only dues-paying members of the Community. The actual number of Jews in Berlin, many of whom remain unaffiliated, is higher and hard to estimate, probably around 18,000 to 20,000.

Policy is in the hands of a council of representatives. Every four years, Community members vote for the 21 representatives, who in turn appoint a five-member executive council to carry out daily decision-making. Since June 1997, the president of the Berlin Community has been Dr. Andreas Nachama, its first "post-Holocaust" leader.

The offices of the Community organization can be found in three separate locations: the Jewish Community Center at Fasanenstrasse 79–80, containing administrative offices, the press office, the educational department, the main library, Arche Noah kosher restaurant, meeting space, and a Holocaust memorial courtyard. In Joachimstaler Strasse 13, social services, the youth department, the religious affairs department and the rabbis' offices are located. The former offices of the small East Berlin Jewish Community at Oranienburger Strasse 28–31 are also used and contain additional offices of the social services and educational department, a branch of the library, and Cafe Oren restaurant.

Israelitische Synagogen-Gemeinde (Adass Jisroel) zu Berlin
(Israelite Synagogue Community (Adass Yisroel) of Berlin)
*Tucholskystrasse 40 (tel: 281 3135). **Transportation:** U-Bahn line U6 to Oranienburger Tor; S-Bahn line S1 or S2 to Oranienburger Strasse; Tram 1 or*

13 to Oranienburger Strasse; **Open:** Monday–Thursday 9:30am–5:30pm, Friday until 3pm.

The original Berlin Adass Yisroel congregation was founded in 1869 by Orthodox Jews unhappy with what they perceived—correctly— as the increasing liberalization of the official Jewish Community organization. Led by the dynamic Esriel Hildesheimer, who—along with Samson Raphael Hirsch in Frankfurt—was a leader of the neo-Orthodox movement in Germany, it eventually established a strong presence in Berlin with two synagogues, a rabbinical seminary (the first modern Orthodox seminary in Germany), a school, and other services for its members. It was always quite small, however, in relation to the main Jewish Community.

The congregation was destroyed by the Nazis. Some 50 years later, in the late 1980s, Mario Offenberg, the son of a member, reestablished the congregation. Using contacts in East Germany, he was able to regain former Adass Yisroel property, such as their neglected cemetery, which was cleared and refurbished. On the site of their former synagogue and rabbinical seminary, a new prayer hall was dedicated in 1990. In 1991, the congregation opened the kosher Beth Café and, a year later, Kolbo, a small shop offering kosher foods and ritual objects, thereby establishing a high profile in the neighborhood that was once considered the Jewish Quarter of Berlin.

Adass Yisroel also runs an outreach program for Soviet immigrants and provides, on an irregular basis, Hebrew classes and walking tours of the neighborhood. It claims some 300 members. In 1995, Adass Yisroel was granted legal status by the city government and they are now a legally recognized corporate body, independent of the Community and eligible for state subsidies.

SYNAGOGUES AND SERVICES

The Jewish Community organization maintains six synagogues, most of them renovated buildings dating from before the 1930s. Adass Yisroel has one as well, making a total of seven synagogues in the city. In contrast there were, before the Nazi government, over 80 Community and private synagogues in the city.

Because the Community must represent the several religious tendencies among its members, it designates certain synagogues

Orthodox, others Liberal, and others something of a mix. An Orthodox rabbi and a Liberal rabbi theoretically serve the Community as a whole rather than the congregants of a single synagogue, though usually the Orthodox rabbi officiates at Joachimstaler Synagogue and the Liberal rabbi at Pestalozzistrasse Synagogue. Currently, Rabbi Yitzchak Ehrenberg, an Israeli who has previously worked in Vienna and Munich, serves as the Community's Orthodox rabbi. Officiating primarily at Pestalozzistrasse is Rabbi Walther Rothschild, born in England to a German-Jewish father and trained at London's Leo Baeck College. He has served in Leeds, Vienna, and, most recently, Aruba.

Visiting the synagogues other than during services is a little problematic. Not only will they be closed, but most of them are inaccessible and even hidden from view in inner courtyards. The exterior of the Fraenkelufer Synagogue can be viewed from the street, and you can get a peek at the Rykestrasse Synagogue through a wrought iron gate leading to its courtyard location. You'll have to pray to see the others.

Pestalozzistrasse 14–15

(tel: 313 8411). **Transportation:** *U-Bahn line U7 to Wilmersdorfer Strasse; Buses 101 or 149 to Kantstrasse/Leibnizstrasse.*

This is one of the most popular places of Jewish worship in the city, and probably the best place to go to get a "feel" for a representative Liberal Berlin service. There is an organ and a mixed choir but seating is separate. If you're lucky, you'll be able to hear the Community's long-standing and very popular head cantor, Estrongo Nachama.

The Pestalozzistrasse Synagogue was built in 1911–12 on the initiative of Betty Sophie Jacobsohn, a businesswoman who donated the property on which it stands. It functioned as a private synagogue for several years until it was taken over by the Community in 1919. It was the most important and popular Orthodox synagogue in western Berlin.

Like many Berlin synagogues, it is tucked away discreetly in a courtyard behind an inconspicuous entrance, an old habit that the smaller, private congregations found especially difficult to break. It is built in a Romanesque style, though with the red brick facade and massive form typical of German medieval architecture.

The synagogue was set on fire during the Kristallnacht pogrom, but the blaze was put out by the fire department, which feared that the neighboring buildings would be burned. The interior of the synagogue was only slightly damaged.

The Liberal Pestalozzistrasse Synagogue is one of the city's most popular.

After the Nazi defeat, services resumed here in late summer 1945, with participants sitting on borrowed garden chairs. The building quickly became the center for the remnants of the community—those returning from the camps as well as those who lived underground during the last years of war—who gathered here to ask about relatives and exchange news. In 1947 the synagogue was renovated.

Friday night services in winter at 6pm, during the summer at 7pm. Saturday morning services at 9:30am.

Joachimstaler Strasse 13
*(tel: 884 2030). **Transportation:** U-Bahn line U9 or U15 to Kurfürstendamm; Buses 119, 129, 146 or 219 to Kurfürstendamm.*

This shul offers rigorous Orthodox services and is the only synagogue offering weekday services. Though the room, which dates from 1902, was built as a B'nai B'rith auditorium, it nevertheless manages an inspiring, synagogal look. Massive chandeliers hang from the high ceiling, large tinted windows allow in hushed light, and ornate, rococo stucco plays over the walls.

Services were held here on high holy days as early as the '30s and on a weekly basis after the Kristallnacht pogram in 1938, when most of the city's synagogues were destroyed or damaged. At that time Leo Baeck officiated here. Today Rabbi Ehrenberg, the Community's Orthodox rabbi, serves here.

Every other Saturday morning at 10:30am there's a "beginners" service for those unfamiliar with the Orthodox liturgy.

Friday night services after sundown. Saturday morning services at 9:30am. Weekday shacharit services at 8am Sunday and 7:30am Monday to Friday. Mincha/Maariv services about 30 minutes before nightfall.

Fraenkelufer 10-16

(tel: 614 5131). **Transportation:** *U-Bahn line U1 or U8 to Kottbusser Tor; Bus 141 to Kottbusser Brücke.*

Seventy-five years ago, if you attended services here, you would have entered an imposing, capacious synagogue, beautifully decorated with neo-classical motifs and seating 2,000. That synagogue, dedicated in 1916, was burned out during the Kristallnacht pogrom and later destroyed by Allied bombing.

Today when one refers to the Fraenkelufer Synagogue, it is only to a surviving side wing that once housed the weekday and youth shul. The narrow room, which holds a couple of hundred worshippers at most, is simply outfitted with a minimum of frills and a small wooden ark and bimah. Its high white walls and spare neo-classical columns make it look something like a New England colonial church.

The original synagogue, completed in 1916, was designed by Alexander Beer, who served as in-house architect for the Jewish Community. Beer died in 1944 in Theresienstadt. This structure was the last of three large synagogues built in the second decade of the century to serve the city's rapidly growing Jewish community (the other two were synagogues on Fasanenstrasse and Levetzowstrasse, both now gone).

Though the room is plain, the worshippers who congregate here for Conservative services are a spirited group and there is a refreshing warmth that is sometimes lacking in some of the other Berlin synagogues.

Friday night services at 7pm. Saturday morning services at 9:30am.

Herbartstrasse 26

(tel: 321 2056). **Transportation:** *S-Bahn line S45 or S46 to Witzleben; Buses 149 or 204 to Kuno-Fischer-Strasse.*

The Leo Baeck Synagogue, a small shul with 135 seats, is Berlin's only post-war synagogue, erected in 1981 to serve the residents of the Jeanette Wolff Senior Citizens' Home and the Leo Baeck Old Age Home. It was designed by Hans Wolff Grohmann in a plain and subdued modern style, but it incorporates columns and religious objects from a prayer hall in the pre-war old age home in Iranischen Strasse. The services are Conservative.

Friday night services in winter at 5:30pm, during the summer at 6pm. Saturday morning services at 9:30am.

Rykestrasse 53

(tel: 448 5298). **Transportation:** *U-Bahn line U2 to Senefelderplatz; Tram 1 to Marienburger Strasse.*

This cavernous synagogue is today the largest extant synagogue in Germany, and therein lies a problem: it is too big. One feels slightly

Built in a courtyard, the Rykestrasse Synagogue survived the Kristallnacht pogrom and is now Germany's largest synagogue.

lost in the huge and sparsely filled hall. The handful of worshippers who gather here on Shabbat, in fact, use a small side chapel, and the main synagogue is used only for festivals.Nevertheless, it is a beautiful synagogue that retains much of the original interior. Because of the synagogue's location in a courtyard surrounded by housing, it survived the Kristallnacht pogrom relatively unscathed. And by luck it was not struck by war-time bombing. The ark and bimah are tremendous, ornate affairs of marble and columns and balustrades. Framing the structure is a brightly painted arc of floral designs. The deep balcony, swathed in stone and supported by low Romanesque pedestals, runs along the flanks of the building.

The synagogue was built in 1903–04 by Johann Höniger (who also designed the no-longer-extant Adass Yisroel synagogue on Tucholskystrasse) to serve a Reform congregation. The Romanesque detailing and red-brick facade were typical of the churches of the time, and are indicative of the identification the Jews of Berlin felt with the dominant culture. Like churches, the synagogue contained an organ and a choir loft, a point of distinction for the Reform movement. Men and women originally sat together for services, a practice no longer followed.

In 1940 the building was taken over by the German army and turned into a munitions magazine. The aisles were used as horse stables. In 1953 it was restored and was for many years the only synagogue for the tiny East Berlin Jewish community. Further renovations took place in 1987. It now hosts Conservative services.

Friday night services in winter at 6pm, during the summer at 7pm. Saturday morning services at 9:30am.

Oranienburger Strasse 29

(tel: 345 4364). **Transportation:** U-Bahn line U6 to Oranienburger Tor; S-Bahn line S1 or S2 to Oranienburger Strasse.

The renovated New Synagogue is now primarily occupied by a museum and offices, but one room of the nineteenth-century landmark has been set aside as a prayer room. In the plain room, equipped with a small, simple ark and folding chairs, the Community's only Reform-style services are held. These services—with mixed seating and women on the bimah—have only recently been introduced, a response by the Community board to grassroots demands for an informal, egalitarian service. It's pleasing that services are once again held in the New Synagogue and fitting that there are, as when the New Synagogue was built, reform-style.

Friday night services at 7pm. Saturday morning services at 9:30am. Thursday shacharit service at 7:30am.

Adass Yisroel Synagogue
Tucholskystrasse 40

(tel: 281 3135). **Transportation:** *U-Bahn line U6 to Oranienburger Tor; S-Bahn line S1 or S2 to Oranienburger Strasse; Tram 1 or 13 to Oranienburger Strasse.*
The Adass Yisroel congregation, dissolved by the Nazi government in 1939, was reestablished in Berlin in 1985. Where the pre-war congregation once had its main synagogue, Adass Yisroel again established a place of worship. Now, however, a small room in the former administrative building must suffice.

The original synagogue, built in 1904 by Johann Höniger, who also designed the Rykestrasse synagogue, was located far off the street in a back courtyard and thus was not damaged during the Kristallnacht pogrom. However, services were halted and the congregation was soon outlawed by the Nazis. The synagogue was damaged by Allied bombing during the war and the ruins torn down in 1967. The sole remaining witness is a Star of David carved into the arch leading into the back courtyard that once contained the shul.

Friday night services begin 5pm to 6:30pm, depending upon time of year. Saturday morning services at 9:30am.

OTHER SERVICES

Culture Society services

The independent Jüdische Kulturverein (Jewish Culture Society) hosts Kabbalat Shabbat services every Friday evening in their offices at Oranienburger Strasse 26 (S-Bahn line S1 or S2 to Oranienburger Strasse; Tram 1 or 13 to Oranienburger Strasse). Call the Culture Society offices at 282 6669 for more information.

Egalitarian minyan

A group with a feminist orientation meets every three weeks for an informal shabbat morning service at Oranienburger Strasse 29 (U-Bahn line U6 to Oranienburger Tor; S-Bahn line S1 or S2 to Oranienburger Strasse; Tram 1 or 13 to Oranienburger Strasse). The siddur is cobbled together from several sources, particularly the Reconstructionist prayerbook. Call 441 8102 for information.

Café & Restaurant
Oren אורן

Middle Eastern
and
Vegetarian Specialties

Oranienburger Strasse 28
10117 Berlin
Tel. 030 / 2 82 82 28

Monday to Thursday	12.00pm– 1.00am
Friday	12.00pm– 2.00am
Saturday	10.00am– 2.00am
Sunday	10.00am– 1.00am

ARCHE NOA

Kosher Restaurant

European &
Middle Easten Food

מסעדה כשרה
תיבת נח

PITA · FALAFEL · HUMUS · TACHINA

Tuesdays between 6.30pm and 11pm
we offer a huge buffet for DM 35 per
person. We can also deliver kosher
food for family celebrations.

Jewish Community Center
Fasanenstrasse 79/80
(030) 882 6138

11.30am —3.30pm and 6.30pm—11pm
Shabbat 11.30am—2.30pm

A PLACE TO FORGET ABOUT THE WORLD...

Barcomi's

Kaffeerösterei & Deli

Diverse Sorten vor Ort gerösteter Kaffeebohnen aus aller We
Homemade Bagels, Muffins, Brownies, Cookies, Cakes, Pies

Bergmannstraße 21 - 10961 Berlin-Kreuzberg
Sophienstraße 21 - 10178 Berlin-Mitte
Tel. 030 / 694 81 38 o. / 285 98 363

2 | Restaurants & Stores

Considering that there are about as many Jews in Berlin as in Indianapolis, Indiana, there is a surprisingly large number of Jewish restaurants and shops here. Most of these establishments have sprouted up in the last five years or so, a development due in part to the renewed vigor of Jewish society in Berlin, in part to the support provided by the Jewish Community organization, and in part to a kind of "Jewish chic" in gentile German culture that makes a brush with Yiddishkeit— eating in a kosher café, for example— an "in" activity. The majority of customers, non-Jewish, may not know a mezuzah from a mazel tov, but there is a great interest in things Jewish, particularly when they can be eaten.

Visitors wishing to take home a piece of Jewish Berlin will encounter difficulties: There are no "native" foods or handicrafts. The restaurants here serve Israeli or Eastern European food; religious objects, foodstuffs, gift items, and the like are imported. Perhaps a good history or picture book—or travel guide—is the best souvenir.

■ Berlin's Bagel Battles

Despite its European pedigree, the bagel was next to unknown here until just a few years ago. Since then, this humble roll has experienced an explosion of popularity, and now the city is locked into a veritable battle of the bagels as a handful of cafés, restaurants and bakeries offer competing versions of this quintessential Jewish food. You can sample the offerings at, among others, Barcomi's, Beth Café, Rimon Restaurant, Salomon's Bagels, Bleibtreu 31 (Bleibtreustrasse 31, Charlottenburg; 884 740) and, on Wednesdays and Saturdays until 1pm, the Winterfeldtplatz farmer's market.

RESTAURANTS   KOSHER

Arche Noah
Fasanenstrasse 79–80 (tel: 882 6138). **Transportation:** *U-Bahn line U2 or U9 to Zoologischer Garten or U15 to Uhlandstrasse; S-Bahn line S3, S5, S7 or S9 to Zoologischer Garten; Bus 109, 119, 129 or 219 to Uhlandstrasse.*
Open: *Sunday–Friday 11:30am–3:30pm & 6:30pm–11pm, Saturday 11:30am–3:30pm. Mid-priced.*
Arche Noah is a snug little restaurant—there can't be more than a

dozen tables—located on the top floor of the Jewish Community Center. The oldest kosher restaurant in the city, it's a bit stuffy and old-fashioned, but charming in an old-European kind of way, complete with starched, white tablecloths and dyspeptic waiters. And for a kosher fleishig dinner, it's the only place in town.

You'll find a lot of old favorites—tscholent, kreplach, gefilte fish, brisket of beef, gedempfte chicken—on the long menu, a kind of smorgasbord of grandma's holiday cooking. But Arche Noah also offers a wide selection of Israeli and Middle Eastern dishes. Kosher wine from Israel is available by the glass.

Arche Noah presents a five-course Shabbat menu for DM 50 and, on Tuesdays from 6:30pm, a buffet featuring 30 different dishes from European and Middle Eastern kitchens for DM 35.

Beth Café

Tucholsky Strasse 40 (tel: 281 3135). ***Transportation:*** *U-Bahn line U6 to Oranienburger Tor; S-Bahn line S1 or S2 to Oranienburger Strasse.*
Open: *Sunday–Thursday 11am–10pm, Friday 11am–3pm. Inexpensive.*
Established in 1991, Beth Café has already become something of a landmark in the neighborhood, a popular stop for visitors touring the so-called Jewish Quarter. It's run by the Orthodox Adass Yisroel congregation and offers a kosher meatless menu of light lunchtime meals. In addition to falafel and other Israeli specialties, soups and salads, they also offer, as a nod to the many American tourists who stop in, gefillte fish and bagels and lox (though they're not quite what you're used to at home).

The small café has a somewhat austere atmosphere, although that may just be due to the self-consciousness of the German patrons. In the summer a quiet courtyard garden is open.

Pläzl Imbiss

Passauer Strasse 4 (tel: 217 7506). ***Transportation:*** *U-Bahn line U1, U2 or U15 to Wittenbergplatz; Bus 119, 129, 146 or 219 to Wittenbergplatz.*
This small snack bar, attached to the Pläzl kosher grocery store, offers the weary shopper (it's located just off the busy shopping strip by KaDeWe department store) or visitor a perfect opportunity for a nosh. Bagels, salads, pita bread and the like in a convivial and informal atmosphere. All delicacies served at the Plätzl snack bar are glatt kosher.

Kosher foods and kibbitzing at Pläzl, a spacious grocery store and delicatessen near Ka De We.

KOSHER-STYLE, ISRAELI & OTHERS

Barcomi's

1) Bergmannstrasse 21 (tel: 694 8138). **Transportation:** *U-Bahn line U7 to Gneisenaustrasse; Bus 341 to Marheinekeplatz;* **Open:** *Monday–Saturday 9am–midnight, Sunday & Holidays 10am–midnight. Inexpensive.*

2) Sophienstrasse 21 (in the Sophie-Gips-Höfe) (tel: 285 98363).
Transportation: *U-Bahn line U8 to Weinmeisterstrasse;* **Open:** *Monday– Saturday 9am–10pm, Sunday & Holidays 10am–10pm. Inexpensive.*

Neither of these two comfortable, inexpensive cafés are kosher, but, styled after New York coffee shops, they're pretty close. American Cynthia Barcomi started with the small café on Bergmannstrasse, a tight little place that's proved so popular she recently opened up the larger café and deli in the Sophie-Gips Courtyards to give her many customers some breathing space.

Both locations offer excellent, homemade bagels and the traditional trimmings—cream cheese, lox, and the like. Barcomi's also features other un-German delights such as muffins and brownies. The larger Sophienstrasse location also offers a sandwich menu, a grocery and gourmet food section (with Celestial Seasoning teas, some California wines, and imported up-scale snack foods) and a long, long deli counter with salads, toppings and baked goods.

There's usually a good supply of *New Yorker* and *Time* magazines on hand as well, and the menu, too, is in English. The service, unfortunately, is decidedly German.

Café Oren

Oranienburger Strasse 28 (tel: 282 8228). **Transportation:** *U-Bahn line U6 to Oranienburger Tor, S-Bahn line S1 or S2 to Oranienburger Strasse;*
Open: *Monday–Friday noon–1am, Saturday & Sunday 10am–1am. Mid-priced.*
If any place constitutes a Jewish community "hangout", this is it. Not that it's an insider secret, however: the restaurant, though quite spacious, fills up just about every evening, and on weekends a reservation is advised. Located next door to the New Synagogue, it's well-placed for recuperating after a tramp around the Jewish sites in the neighborhood.

Oren offers a meatless—but not kosher—menu featuring fish

Next door to the New Synagogue, Café Oren is a popular stop for Israeli and Middle Eastern meals.

dishes (among them matjes in several formats), vegetarian casseroles and pastas, and middle-eastern specialties such as baba ganoush and humus. You can drink Israeli too: several Israeli wines are offered as well as Maccabee beer. In the summer there's dining al fresco in the courtyard.

Rimon Restaurant

Oranienburger Strasse 26 (tel: 283 84032). **Transportation:** *U-Bahn line U6 to Oranienburger Tor, S-Bahn line S1 or S2 to Oranienburger Strasse.* **Open:** *Daily 10am–2am. Mid-priced.*

The latest and most ambitious kosher-style restaurant in the city. It occupies two floors of an airy and spacious location in the Jewish Communication Center, just down the block from the New Synagogue. Not quite kosher, this vegetarian restaurant offers excellent and authentic Israeli specialties and Eastern European favorites such as gefillte fish, kreplach, latkes, and bagels. Fish is a specialty of the house. Around the corner, a take-out snack counter is attached to the restaurant. Rimon also offers a kosher catering service.

Salomon Bagels

1) Joachimstaler Strasse 13 (tel: 821 0404). **Transportation:** *U-Bahn line U1 or U15 to Kurfürstendamm; Bus 119, 129, 146 or 219 to Joachimstaler Strasse.* **Open:** *Monday–Friday 9am–8pm, Saturday 9am–4pm. Inexpensive.*
2) Potsdamer Platz Arkaden. **Transportation:** *U-Bahn line U2 to Potsdamer Platz; Bus 248 to Potsdamer Platz.* **Open:** *Monday–Friday 9am–8pm, Saturday 9am–4pm. Inexpensive.*

For Andreas Pfeffer, owner and mentor of Salomon's, the bagel is a spiritual object. Its round shape is a metaphor for wholeness and reconciliation, the boiling and baking required to produce it a symbol for the union of water and fire. "Wisdom that one can eat," is his slogan. Whether transcendent or not, however, the bagels baked here are large, fresh and delicious.

The Joachimstaler Strasse Salomon's is pocket-sized but cheery, with lox-colored walls and a huge golden chandelier poised over the glass vitrine. It's a *steh-café*, meaning there's standing only at the high tables, which is a shame because it's the kind of place you would like to linger in while noshing. In addition to six varieties of bagels, which can be bought by the dozen, Salomon's offers small sandwiches, cakes, and even homemade New York-style cheesecake.

Salomon's new branch in the Potsdamer Platz Arkaden shopping mall, part of the Daimler-Benz headquarters complex, is a much larger, much more comfortable affair. Chairs and sofas allow you finally to sit while enjoying a Salomon bagel, and an expanded menu makes the lingering that much more tempting.

Tabuna Restaurant and Café

Alt-Moabit 59 (tel: 390 7040). **Transportation:** *U-Bahn line U9 to Turmstrasse, Bus 245 or 341 to Gotzkowskystrasse.* **Open:** *Daily noon–midnight. Mid-priced.*
The restaurant's pride and joy, a stone tabuna oven, is set proudly by the front door to warm and welcome customers. It is, according to the owner, the only one in Europe, imported with loving care from Israel, and it does deliver: the huge pitas that emerge from its depths are crisp and delicate and delivered warm to your table.

There's a generous offering of the appropriate fixings for accompaniment—kebabs of several varieties, falafel, kubba, humous, and the like. In addition, Tabuna offers continental and pasta dishes.

The picture windows lining one side offer a view of the meandering (though not quite bucolic) Spree River and there's a terrace for dining outside when the weather is good. On weekends there's often live Israeli and Russian folk music.

BOOKSTORES

Literaturhandlung

Joachimstaler Strasse 13 (tel: 882 4250). **Transportation:** *U-Bahn line U1 or U15 to Kurfürstendamm; Bus 119, 129, 146 or 219 to Joachimstaler Strasse.*
Berlin's only Jewish bookstore. Literaturhandlung—the name means simply Literature Store—is something of an oasis, one of the few places in Berlin one can go and be thoroughly immersed in things Jewish. It's not large, but it's extremely well-stocked and a great browser's bookstore. Open since 1993, this is the latest branch of a store with outlets in Munich and Vienna.

About 10% of the offerings are in English. Strong suits include European Jewish history, books on the Third Reich and Jews under Nazism, and literature (the latter, however, all in German). Just about anything in print on Jewish Berlin can be found here too, but the vast majority, of course, is in German. There's a good-sized

Yiddish section and lots in Hebrew.

If the printed word leaves you cold, you can find plenty of CDs and cassette tapes: Israeli pop, Yiddish and klezmer music, and cantorial singing. Literaturhandlung also sells calendars, cards, Jewish newspapers and magazines from Germany and abroad, as well as ritual objects such as mezuzim and kippot. Anything in the store is also available by mail order.

Kiepert's

Hardenbergstrasse 4–5 (tel: 311 0090). **Transportation:** *U-Bahn line U2 to Ernst-Reuter-Platz; Bus 145 or 245 to Ernst-Reuter-Platz.*

Berlin's largest bookstore contains a surprisingly ample Judaica section, with a thoughtful selection of books, many in English. The section is stocked and supervised by an independent distributor of Judaica, Micaela Weiss (see the Judaica section below) and she brings a practiced eye to the selection. She emphasizes theology and liturgy—you can pick up an English-language Siddur here, for example, if you've left yours at home—but there are also English-language best-sellers, some fiction, and even a few children's books. You'll also find a selection of software: Hebrew language instruction, Talmud exegesis, Torah study, and more. Elsewhere in Kiepert's, there's an English-language department with a solid section on German and Berlin history and the occasional book on some aspect of German Jewry.

FOODSTUFFS

Kolbo

Auguststrasse 77/78 (tel: 281 31 35). **Transportation:** *U-Bahn line U6 to Oranienburger Tor; S-Bahn line S1 or S2 to Oranienburger Strasse.*

This small shop, affiliated with the Adass Yisroel Orthodox congregation, stocks a good selection of kosher foodstuffs, wine, and ritual objects. Manischewitz and Rokeach are in ample supply of course, but Kolbo also stocks some unexpected items, such as cosmetics and personal hygiene products from Israel and frozen kosher poultry from France. They have an excellent stock of kosher wines from several well-regarded Israeli wineries. They bake their own bagels, challah, and cakes and make their own gefilte fish, a surprise for those raised on Manischewitz. Before Passover they sell fresh horseradish, and during the summer Galil Israeli ice cream.

Kolbo also offers some inedibles: there's a selection of books (all in German) and a number of klezmer and cantorial CDs. Tucked in a corner of the store is a display case of ritual objects and jewelry.

Kosher Deli

Goethestrasse 61 (tel: 315 09243). **Transportation:** *U-Bahn line U2 or U7 to Bismarck Strasse or line U7 to Wilsmersdorfer Strasse;*
Open: *Monday–Thursday 9am–5:30pm, Friday 9am–1pm.*

Berlin's only kosher butcher. The fresh beef, lamb, and poultry stem from organically raised, free-roaming local livestock. All meat is koshered on the premises, supervised by an Israeli shochet resident in Berlin and certified by Rabbi Ehrenberg of the Jewish Community organization. Bright white and brand-spanking new—the shop replaces an older kosher butcher here that was looking decidedly down at the heels—it also features a delicatessen counter, kosher staples, and a small snack bar.

Pläzl

Passauer Str. 4 (tel: 217 7506). **Transportation:** *U-Bahn line U1, U2 or U15 to Wittenbergplatz; Bus 119, 129, 146 or 219 to Wittenbergplatz.*

In contrast to many other Jewish spots in the city, Pläzl is not retiring: a large sign in German and Yiddish hangs over a display window full of Israeli wine and food. It's a refreshing assurance. Co-owner Uri Gabrielli hopes that the store will develop into a meeting place and social center for the Jewish community and visitors.

There's a large array of kosher foodstuffs with a distinctly Israeli bent, not only matzah but also potato chips and candy bars, instant noodles, falafel mix, and other kosher convenience foods. Traditional eastern European foods, such as gefilte fish, herring, lox, and kosher sausage can be found here as well. Pläzl devotes an entire back room to kosher wines (Carmel and Yarden among others) and spirits, the best selection in the city. In front there's a kosher delicatessen counter and snack bar.

Schalom

Wielandstrasse 43 (tel: 312 1131). **Transportation:** *S-Bahn line S3, S5, S7, S9, or S75 to Savignyplatz; Bus 101 or 149 to Kantstrasse/Leibnizstrasse.*

Schalom is the oldest, and was for a long, long time the only kosher food store in Berlin. Since 1965 it has been offering Israeli and

American products from margarine to macaroons. Specialties include Sabra liqueur, Carmel and Golan wines, and frozen poultry.

A little worn at the edges, it has a kind of relaxed charm, intimate and haphazard. The store is actually located in the building's inner courtyard, and you'll find the entrance through the driveway. If you're being very careful on German soil, it allows for discreet shopping.

JUDAICA

Tabularium

*Grosse Hamburger Strasse 28 (tel: 308 72095). **Transportation:** U-Bahn line U8 to Weinmeisterstrasse; Tram 1 or 13 to Monbijouplatz.*

Basically a toy and gift shop, Tabularium devotes a section of the store and one window to Judaica, jewelry, and books. The wares includes yarmulkes, prayer shawls, silver candelabras, kiddush cups, mezuzot, books (German only) and the like. Though modest by New York or London standards, it is, however, one of the best selections in the city.

Jüdische Galerie

*Oranienburger Strasse 31 (tel: 282 8623). **Transportation:** U-Bahn line U6 to Oranienburger Tor, S-Bahn line S1 or S2 to Oranienburger Strasse.*

***Open:** Monday–Thursday 12:30pm–6:30pm; Friday 1pm–5pm; Sunday 11am–3pm.*

A small and somewhat chaotic art gallery next door to the New Synagogue that usually shows works from young Jewish artists from the former Soviet Union. Some handcrafted religious objects, such as ceramic menorahs and Kiddush cups, are offered for sale, making this the only place where you can purchase "native" handicrafts. Posters and postcards, for those on a limited budget, are available too.

Micaela R. Weiss

Tel: 313 8725

Ms. Weiss is an independent distributor and retailer of Judaica, books, CDs and cassettes, and software. She manages the Judaica book section in Kiepert's, Berlin's largest general bookstore, and sets up a table as well at special events and Jewish functions. Her firm is perhaps the only source in Berlin for items such as tallit and teffilin.

MISCELLANEOUS

Jewish Communication Center

Oranienburger Strasse 26 (tel: 323 0901). **Transportation:** *U-Bahn line U6 to Oranienburger Tor or S-Bahn line S1 or S2 to Oranienburger Strasse.*

The Jewish Communication Center is a kind of Jewish mini-mall put up by a private developer a few doors down from the New Synagogue on Oranienburger Strasse. In addition to a kosher-style restaurant (Rimon), it includes office space for Jewish business and organizations, and short-term apartment rentals for visitors. Its location just down the street from the New Synagogue is sure to act as a further draw for the neighborhood.

Bank Leumi

Europa-Center, Breitscheidplatz (tel: 2549 3151). **Transportation:** *U-Bahn line U9 or U15 to Kurfürstendamm; Bus 119, 129, 146 or 219 to Europa-Center.*

This Israeli bank has an office here for information and consultation only; it is not a full-service banking outlet.

Bank Hapoalim

Katharinenstrasse 8 (tel: 890 28 50). **Transportation:** *Bus 110, 119, 129 or 219 to Kurfürstendamm/Joachim-Friedrich-Strasse.*

Another Israeli bank with representation in Berlin.

El-Al Airlines

Friedrichstrasse 95 (tel: 201 3745). **Transportation:** *U-Bahn line U6 or S-Bahn line S1, S2, S3, S7, S9, S25 or S75 to Friedrichstrasse; Bus 100, 147 or 348 to Unter den Linden/Friedrichstrasse.*

A branch office of the Israeli airlines. El-Al flys non-stop out of Berlin to Israel three times a week.

3 | Festivals & Cultural Events

Much of the life of Jewish Berlin revolves around annual festivals and events, the most important of which are listed here. There are plenty of other goings-on—concerts, children's theater, lectures and seminars, and the like, that occur irregularly. A detailed monthly schedule of those events sponsored by the Jewish Community can be found (in German and Russian) in their newsletter, *Jüdisches Berlin*. The Jewish Culture Society also sponsors a full schedule of events, which is listed (in German and Russian) in their monthly *Jüdische Korrespondenz* newsletter. Independent events of Jewish interest are often listed in the city's three program magazines, *Tip*, *Zitty*, and *Berlin Programm* (all in German). Where no other phone number is noted, call the Jewish Community office at 880 280 for more information.

SEPTEMBER

Rosh Hashana & Yom Kippur
As in every Jewish community, seating for the High Holy Days can be tight. However, in Berlin there is always room in the huge Ryke-strasse Synagogue, the best bet for visitors and non-members. Services are Conservative (and seating is separate). For more information on seating and tickets for the Community synagogues, call 880 28124. For tickets at Adass Yisroel services, contact their office at 281 3135.

NOVEMBER

9: Kristallnacht Pogrom Commemoration
Every year the Jewish Community holds a memorial service on the anniversary of the Kristallnacht pogrom. The Community's cantor, Estrongo Nachama, sings and local politicians give speeches. Other organizations, such as peace groups, concentration camp survivor organizations and student classes also conduct various commemorative events and vigils.

Jüdische Kulturtage
(Jewish Culture Days)

This festival, sponsored by the Jewish Community organization, is one of the high points of Berlin's Jewish calendar. It features a month-long program of lectures, readings, seminars, film and music. Each year the festival focuses (loosely) on a different theme—past years have examined Jewish culture in Paris, Jerusalem, Southern California, New York, and Berlin. The festival is capped each year by a lively concert at the Jewish Community Center on Fasanenstrasse. The program is published about a month in advance and can be picked up at the Community Center. Events often sell out, so tickets are best purchased early.

DECEMBER

Chanukah Ball

The Jewish Community organization hosts an annual Chanukah Ball featuring a sit-down dinner, music, dancing and a wheel of fortune. The Jewish Culture Society (282 6669) also holds a somewhat more casual Chanukah Ball with food, music and dancing.

For children there are Chanukah parties sponsored by various groups with music, dancing, and storytelling, and the Community organization hosts a candle lighting outside the Community center on the first night of the festival.

JANUARY

Tu B'shvat Ball

A yearly gathering at the Jewish Community Center, with music and a sumptuous buffet, sponsored by the Simon Dubnow chapter of the B'nai B'rith.

27: Gedenktag für die Opfer des Nationalsozialismus
(Remembrance Day for Victims of National Socialism)

On January 27, 1945, the Soviet Red Army reached Auschwitz and freed the remaining prisoners of the death factory. Fifty-one years later, the German parliament declared this date to be a day of remembrance for all victims—Jews and Gentiles—of the Nazi terror. Politicians lay wreaths and make speeches, though the day has yet to become securely established as a memorial day.

The inner courtyard of the Jewish Community House on Fasanenstrasse serves as a setting for many commemorative events; this is a memorial service for the anniversary of the liberation of Auschwitz.

MARCH

Purim Ball
The *Jugendzentrum* (Youth Center) hosts a Purim party for youngsters featuring music, games, and food. Costumes are encouraged.

WIZO Bazaar
This annual fundraiser for the Women's International Zionist Organization (the international equivalent of Hadassah) has something of a high-society character, attracting luminaries of the Jewish Community and local politicians.

APRIL

Passover Seders
The Jewish Community organization, Adass Yisroel (281 3135), and the Jewish Culture Society (282 6669) all host Orthodox seders on the first and second nights. Visitors are welcome, but seating is limited (and sometimes expensive) and prior arrangements must be made.

MAY

Yom Ha'Shoah

The B'nai B'rith Youth Organization has, for the last several years, organized a public reading—part vigil, part yizkor—of the names of all 55,696 Berlin Jews murdered by the Nazis. For more than 24 hours the names ring out. The gathering has taken place in various locations; call the Community for more information.

JUNE

Jewish Film Festival

The *Jüdische Volkshochschule* (Jewish Adult Education Program) puts together a week-long Jewish Film Festival every year. Loosely grouped around a theme—past years have featured, for example, Jewish humor in film and Jewish women in film—the festival presents well-known classics and obscure gems, many in English. For more information, call the *Volkshochschule* office at 880 28236.

Jewish Street Festival

In 1997 the first Jewish Street Festival in Berlin took place, a striking example of the new self-confidence and high profile of Jews in the city. Sponsored by the Jewish Community and the Federal Union of Jewish Students in Germany, the lively festival features booths with food from local restaurants and information from various Jewish organizations, a stage with live music, and contests and prizes.

4 | Groups & Organizations

The "packed suitcase" syndrome—the feeling of many post-war Jews that they were not settled permanently in Germany—kept the level of social activism relatively low for many years. Several groups were formed under the auspices of the Jewish Community, but there were few grassroots organizations. In the past ten years or so, however, the suitcases have disappeared. There are many new groups exploring Jewish culture, seeking reform, feminist and egalitarian religious paths, projecting a new political determination, or sometimes just socializing and having fun.

The Community, responding to its larger and younger clientele, now sponsors a diverse offering of groups: a chess club, a children's choir, a Red Army veterans' group, a computer club, and others. The new status of Berlin as capital city of a reunified Germany has attracted new institutions and international groups. Their numbers are likely to increase when the government moves its operations from Bonn to Berlin over the next several years.

INSTITUTIONS

Israeli Consulate
Schinkelstrasse 10 (tel: 893 2203). **Transportation:** *Bus 110 or 129 to Bismarckplatz;* **Open:** *Monday–Thursday 9am–noon; Friday 9am–11am.*
The Israeli consulate is located far away from the center of town in a corner of the Wilmersdorf district. Heading up the office since February, 1997 is Miryam Shomrat.

Stiftung Centrum Judaicum—Neue Synagoge
(Centrum Judaicum—New Synagogue Foundation)
Oranienburger Str. 28 (tel: 284 01250).
In the late 1980s, the communist government of East Germany agreed to renovate the New Synagogue on Oranienburger Strasse. This once grand building had remained a ruined hulk for half a century, and it was decided to turn the structure into a monument and Jewish cultural center of some kind. The Stiftung Centrum Judai-

No longer principally a place of worship, the New Synagogue is now a museum and the seat of the Centrum Judaicum Foundation.

cum—Neue Synagoge was set up in 1988 to pursue these goals. There was no provision for this kind of independent foundation under East German law, and a special decree had to be enacted. The project was officially inaugurated on November 10, 1988 at a memorial gathering for the 50th anniversary of the Kristallnacht pogrom, with Erich Honecker, the communist head of state, in attendance.

The renovation of the surviving portion of the synagogue was completed in 1995, long after Honecker's office and country had ceased to exist. A sensitive and successful renovation has transformed the structure into an exhibition space, cultural center, lecture hall, and tourist attraction. It has become an almost mandatory stop for visitors exploring Jewish Berlin and school classes learning about "lost" Jewish history. The New Synagogue is again, as it was before the war, one of the city's major landmarks.

The foundation itself, in addition to its work in maintaining and administering the former synagogue, also sponsors research, organizes lectures and seminars, maintains an archive, and produces publications on the history of Jewish Berlin.

Zentralrat der Juden in Deutschland
(Central Council of Jews in Germany)
Tucholskystr. 9 (tel: 282 8714).

This is the central umbrella group for all the Jewish community organizations throughout Germany (there are 72 of them). It coordinates policies and serves as a united voice for the rights and interests of the Jewish communities on a national level. The current head is Ignatz Bubis, who, though sometimes critical of official foreign policy and immigration law, enjoys a close working relationship with the German government. The building on Tucholskystrasse once housed the prestigious College for the Science of Judaism, and the council's tenancy restores a Jewish presence to the historic structure.

INDEPENDENT & GRASSROOTS ORGANIZATIONS

Anti-Defamation Forum
Oranienburger Strasse 31 (tel: 283 6552).

An activist organization and a research and documentation center dedicated to fighting anti-Semitism and racism. A main goal is to provide a clearinghouse for the dissemination of information about anti-Semitic incidents, neo-Nazi groups, Holocaust denial publications, and the like.

B'nai B'rith
Simon Dubnow Loge (tel: 881 1917).
Janusz Korczak Loge (tel: c/o Jewish Community 880 280).
Raoul Wallenberg Loge (tel: 885 9450).
Leo Baeck B'nai B'rith Youth Organization (tel: 282 9869).

There are three Berlin lodges (*Logen* in German) of B'nai B'rith, the fraternal organization: the Simon Dubnow Loge, the Janusz Korczak Loge, and the Raoul Wallenberg Loge.

Something like the *landsmanshaftn* of the New World, they tend to be organized along national lines: The Simon Dubnow Loge is made up in large part of Russians and the Janusz Korczak Loge is comprised principally of those of Polish background. The Raoul Wallenberg Loge, somewhat less definable by nationality, attracts a younger membership. While many of their activities are social in nature, they also sometimes participate in political and outreach activities. The Raoul Wallenberg Loge, for example, annually awards the Raoul Wallenberg Prize to international figures active in the fight against anti-Semitism.

In addition, there is a B'nai B'rith Youth Organization chapter, the Leo Baeck Gruppe. They have organized a campaign against racism and anti-Semitism called Unite & Act, one of the few pro-active Jewish initiatives in Berlin. They have held demonstrations, concerts, and commemoration ceremonies with the goal of reaching beyond the Jewish population and creating awareness and alliances with non-Jewish youths.

Bund der Verfolgten des Naziregimes
(Union of Those Persecuted by the Nazi Regime)
Mommsenstrasse 27 (tel: 324 2632).

This group of resistance fighters and others persecuted for political and religious reasons publishes a newsletter (available at the Jewish Community Center) and sponsors various memorial and educational events.

Bundesverband der Jüdischen Studenten in Deutschland
(Federal Union of Jewish Students in Germany)
Joachimsthaler Strasse 13 (tel: 885 51303).

Open to Jewish students from 18 to 30 years old, the BJSD is a spirited group involved in a wide range of educational, political and social events such as educational seminars, retreats, holiday celebrations and parties. They host occasional Shabbat dinners where visiting Jewish students are welcomed. The BJSD was founded in 1968 and has about 1,500 members.

Club Massoret
Passauer Strasse 4 (tel: c/o Jewish Community 880 280).

A group dedicated to furthering Jewish education and practice, it meets every Sunday afternoon in the Jewish Community rooms at Passauer Strasse. Informal talks and discussions on religious themes, accompanied by coffee and cake, are held; German and Russian are spoken.

Deutsch-Israelische Gesellschaft
(German-Israel Society)

Ernst-Ring-Strasse 4 (tel: 803 4376).

An organization that promotes friendship, understanding and, principally, business relations between Germany and Israel. It publishes a newsletter, organizes group trips to Israel, and sponsors events, which are usually speeches by government officials or business experts.

Frauengruppe
(Women's Club)

Oranienburger Strasse 29 (tel: 284 01280).

This group, which was founded in East Berlin before reunification, is still made up primarily of women from the eastern part of the city. It offers a lively and informal program of lectures, discussions, and concerts centering on Jewish history, culture, and tradition.

Jüdischer Kulturverein
(Jewish Culture Society)

Oranienburger Strasse 26 (tel: 282 6669).

The Jewish Culture Society is an independent group that offers a varied program of cultural, educational, religious, and social events. The Culture Society has its roots in a small group of Jews in East Berlin who got together in 1986 for cultural activities, to celebrate holidays, and to rediscover their Jewish roots. Many had only recently developed an interest in Judaism, many were not halachically Jewish, others had been turned off by the purely religious orientation of the official East Berlin Jewish Community. After reunification, when the small official East Berlin Jewish Community was subsumed by its western counterpart, the Culture Society decided to continue as an independent group.

The Culture Society maintains its "Eastern" flavor, with a radical edge to many of its activities and a special outreach to Russian emigrants. Many of its members hail from the former Soviet Union, and many events are conducted in Russian or with Russian themes. At the same time, the group has a strong relationship with the Lubavitcher Chassidic movement, which supplies visiting rabbis and provides religious instruction. Anyone, Jew or Gentile, can become a member and participate in activities; the atmosphere is informal and friendly. The club welcomes English-speaking visitors.

The Culture Society hosts Kabbalat Shabbat services in German and Russian and maintains a lively program of concerts, lectures, and discussions. They boast a youth group and a choir. They also publish a bimonthly newsletter, *Jüdische Korrespondenz*, (in German and Russian editions) that offers news and notes and, often, an iconoclastic view of the Jewish community.

Jüdischer Runder Tisch Deutschland
(Jewish Round Table)
Tel: c/o the Jewish Culture Society 282 6669.
An informal group organized in 1992 and dedicated to inter-Jewish dialog among independent groups throughout Germany. Every three months, member organizations (in Berlin they include the Jewish Culture Society and Adass Yisroel) and unaffiliated individuals gather in a different German city to discuss common problems and concerns.

Kesher, Israelis in Berlin
Tel: c/o Jewish Community 880 280.
A social group of Israelis away from home. They meet regularly to chat in Hebrew, enjoy Israeli culture, exchange news, and trade memories. The group has a loose membership of about 150. There are probably somewhere around 500-1,000 Israelis living in the German capital.

Meshulash
Tel: 396 1789.
Composed of young Jews and non-Jews from many countries, this group is involved in a range of political and cultural projects dealing with Jewish identity and history. Their activities are varied, from participation in demonstrations to organizing museum exhibitions.

Organisation der Jüdischen Ärzte und Psychologen in Berlin
(Organization of Jewish Doctors and Psychologists in Berlin)
Tel: 315 8014.
Professional group that holds discussions on relevant themes.

Pnujim w Pnujot Jüdischer Singles-Club
Tel: 313 1145.
A group of singles dedicated to mingling and matchmaking. Every

Thursday, at 6:30pm at Passauer Strasse 4, they host a get-together with entertainment and refreshment and attract a lively, middle-aged crowd.

TuS (Turn- und Sport-Club) Makkabi
(Maccabee Gymnastic and Sport Club)

Passauer Strasse 4 (tel: 218 4708).
Originally founded in 1898 (under the name Bar Kochba) as the first Jewish gymnastics and sports club in the world and destroyed by the Nazis, this sports group was reorganized in 1970 and now counts among its offerings soccer, swimming, tennis, ping pong, gymnastics, volleyball, boxing and sailing. The club holds frequent tournaments and competitions, and often travel to play with and against other Jewish and non-Jewish sports teams.

Yachad

c/o Mann-o-Meter, Motzstrasse 5 (tel: 216 3336).
The Berlin branch of a nationwide group of gay and lesbian Jews dedicated to strengthening gay and Jewish identity. In addition to political activities and lobbying, they also gather regularly to celebrate Jewish holidays.

INTERNATIONAL ORGANIZATIONS

American Jewish Committee

Leipziger Platz 15 (tel: 226 5940).
The venerable advocacy and human rights group opened an office in the city in 1997 to conduct research, publish reports and sponsor academic conferences and symposia. The Ramer Center for German-Jewish Relations, as the office is officially known, also houses an English-language library focusing on American Jewry. The Committee has lately been involved in lobbying the German government to provide pensions for Holocaust survivors living in Eastern Europe and the former Soviet Union.

Chabad Lubavitch Berlin

Ballenstedter Strasse 16a (tel: 891 2531).
In 1996, at the invitation of the Jewish Community organization, the Lubavitcher Chasidic movement established a Chabad House here. As with the several hundred other Chabad centers around the

world, the Berlin house has as its goal increasing religious knowledge and participation among Jews. Heading up the center here is the energetic Brooklyn-born Rabbi Yehuda Teichtel and his Israeli wife Leah. They teach classes, sponsor festival seders and parties, conduct weddings and circumcisions, and are generally available for questions or help of any kind. They publish a weekly newsletter of commentary on the Torah portion.

The Ronald S. Lauder Foundation

Oranienburger Strasse 65 (tel: 283 6823).
A new Berlin office of the American foundation established to support and revitalize eastern European Jewish communities. Here in Berlin, the Foundation focuses on Jewish education and identity and is working to establish a teaching college for Jewish educators.

Wizo Berlin

Joachimstaler Str. 13 (tel: 882 5589).
This is the Berlin branch of the Women's International Zionist Organization, which serves as a support group for educational and social services in Israel (Hadassah is the counterpart in the United States). Wizo Berlin has helped to sponsor various social and educational projects in Israel and conducts numerous charity events here in Berlin. Their annual fundraising bazaar has become an established date on the Berlin society calendar.

Zionistische Organisation in Deutschland

Joachimstaler Str. 13 (tel: 881 7797).
What better place, many would say, for a Zionist group than Germany? Though tracing its roots back to the original pre-war German Zionist organization, this branch was established in Berlin only in 1954. There is also an active Zionist Youth Group. The Jewish Community here is strongly committed to Israel as the Zionist homeland.

5 | Social & Educational Services

In keeping with the traditionally strong Jewish emphasis on social work and community support, there is a much larger social services network than one might expect given the relatively small number of Jewish inhabitants in the city. The Community has succeeded in building an infrastructure that extends just about from womb to tomb, offering educational opportunities, health services, job counseling, welfare support, and social, cultural and religious activities.

The value of this broad structure has been shown in the last decade or so when large numbers of Russian Jews, many in need of language classes, vocational counseling and training, and religious instruction arrived in the city. Although integration has not always been smooth, the necessary services were usually available when needed.

The Community also supports a great number of social and educational activities and groups, especially for children. These include dance groups, choruses, lecture and concert series, musical instruction, ceramics classes, computer training, a chess club, and many more. A look at the Berlin Community's newsletter, *Jüdisches Berlin*, gives you an idea of the wide and lively array of activities.

EDUCATION

Kindertagesstätte der Jüdische Gemeinde (Jewish Community Child Care Center/Kindergarten)
Delbrückstrasse 8 (tel: 891 6748).
The roots of the child care center/kindergarten reach back to 1946, when 15 children were brought together in one room in the Jewish Community offices on Joachimstaler Strasse. The modern building on Delbrückstrasse, dating from 1971, was the first new Jewish school structure built in Germany since the Holocaust. Over 200 children, ages two-and-a-half to six years, attend. For the many children of assimilated Russian immigrants, the center often provides a child's first introduction to Jewish life.

Heinz Galinski Grundschule
(Heinz Galinski Elementary School)

Waldschulallee 73 (tel: 301 1940).

Named after the longtime post-war president of the Berlin Jewish Community, this school was opened on September 15, 1995. Designed by Israeli architect Zvi Hecker, the unusual structure unfolds in a dramatic and dynamic design based on a sunflower. Some 240 students, ages six to ten years, Jews and non-Jews, attend the school. They are instructed in the state-mandated secular curriculum and also receive religious and Hebrew instruction.

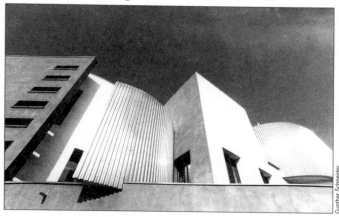

The Heinz Galinski elementary school, named after the long-serving postwar leader of the Jewish Community, features a striking design by Israeli architect Zvi Hecker.

Oberschule/Realschule
(Secondary School)

Grosse Hamburger Strasse 27 (tel: 238 5781).

A Jewish school first appeared on this site in 1863, and the present high school can trace its roots (a little tenuously) to the Jewish Free School opened in 1778 by David Friedländer and Isaac Daniel Itzig, the first school in Germany to combine religious instruction with a secular education. Reopened on August 6, 1993, the school now serves a student body of some 350, not all Jewish, and one-third Russian-born. In addition to secular subjects (the school is an accredited institution), students learn Hebrew, Jewish history and law, and religious practices.

Jüdische Volkshochschule
(Jewish Adult Education Program)

Fasanenstrasse 79/80 (tel: 880 28 263).

Founded in 1962, this adult education program is one of the most successful and popular offerings of the Jewish Community. Its classes, lectures and special events attract large audiences from both the Community and Berlin's non-Jewish population. Each of the school's yearly trimesters features religious instruction; Hebrew, German, Yiddish, and Russian language courses; history surveys, and other classes of Jewish interest. Special programs, such as discussion panels on current events and Jewish history, readings by authors, concerts, and an annual Jewish Film Festival, are offered as well. A brochure with current offerings is available from the Jewish Community Center.

Berlin Tourismus Marketing

The Jewish Community Center on Fasanenstrasse serves as the nerve center of Berlin's Jewish Community.

Jüdische Jugendzentrum
(Jewish Youth Center)
Joachimstaler Strasse 13 (tel: 880 281 23).

The Youth Center is located in the courtyard behind the Community administrative offices on Joachimstaler Strasse. Here a group of young men and women aged 16 to 30 years organize festivities for Chanukah, Purim, and other holidays; host dances; take field trips; hold discussions; and even publish a newsletter.

Sporthalle der Jüdischen Gemeinde
(Jewish Community Gymnasium)
Oranienburger Strasse 31.

A new gymnasium and sports center in a back courtyard beside the New Synagogue, this spacious, glass-walled hall provides facilities for the Jewish school around the corner on Grosse Hamburger Strasse and the Makkabi sports club. It is open to students from some of the nearby state schools as well.

Moses Mendelssohn Zentrum für europäisch-jüdische Studien
(The Moses Mendelssohn Center for European-Jewish Studies)
Rembrandtstr. 27, Potsdam (tel: 0331 280 940).

Affiliated with Potsdam University, this university-level academic center was opened in June 1994 to offer a degree program for Jewish Studies and is the only institution in Germany where such a degree can be obtained. In addition, the Center carries out research projects, hosts conferences, and funds publications in the areas of religious studies, philosophy, regional history, literary history, and the study of anti-Semitism, among other topics. In 1996, 55 students were enrolled.

LIBRARIES

Jüdische Gemeinde Bibliothek
(Jewish Community Library)
Fasanenstr. 79-80 (tel: 880 28235).

A compact but excellent library of some 60,000 volumes that contains a great deal of material in English. There are strong sections on Germany and east European Jewry as well as the Third Reich and the Holocaust. English-language newspapers include the *Jerusalem Post* and London's *Jewish Chronicle*. A notable feature is the excellent collection of important German-language Jewish newspapers and periodicals from the nineteenth and early twentieth century, available on microfilm.

In addition, the library has a copy of the Berlin Memorial Book for the Jewish Victims of National Socialism, which lists the names of all Berlin Jews murdered in the Holocaust. A smaller branch library, which along with a more modest holding of books also contains a CD and video collection, is located at Oranienburger Str. 28 (tel: 284 01227).

Haus der Wannsee-Konferenz Bibliothek (Wannsee Conference House Library)
Am Grossen Wannsee 56-58 (tel: 805 0010).
The memorial and museum housed in the villa that hosted the Wannsee conference contains an archive with a comprehensive library of materials about the Holocaust, German Jewry, and National Socialism. Much of the collection of 14,000 volumes is in English, and the library also contains films, documentaries, and a collection of video testimonies of Holocaust survivors (produced in cooperation with the Moses Mendelssohn Center). The archive is not, however, a lending library, so all materials must be used on the premises.

The Dr. Hans Adler Library of the American Jewish Committee
Leipziger Platz 15 (tel: 226 5940).
Housed in the Berlin offices of the American Jewish Committee, this library of English-language books focuses on American Jewry and the history of Judaism in the United States. It is small—only about 1500 volumes—but well-focused and comfortable. It is not a lending library and appointments should be made before visiting.

SOCIAL SERVICES

Esra (Hilfe für NS-Verfolgte und deren Kinder) (Help for the Nazi-persecuted and their children)
Iranische Strasse 2-4 (tel: 491 9491).
This group offers counseling and therapy to victims of the National Socialists and their children, regardless of nationality or religion. They organize individual and group therapy sessions, hold workshops and seminars, and have a drop-in center in the Jewish Hospital, Iranische Str. 2-4, Mondays to Thursdays, 2pm–5pm.

Herman-Strauss-Hospital
Iranische Strasse 2-4 (tel: 492 3061).
Located on the grounds of the Jewish Hospital, this nursing home offers a Jewish environment for chronically ill patients. Jewish festivals are celebrated and kosher food served.

Jewish Hospital
Iranische Strasse 2-4 (tel: 49 941).
The Jewish Hospital can trace back its history some 240 years to 1756, when a small infirmary was built by the Community on Oranienburger Strasse. Though now a non-denominational public institution, the 400-bed hospital retains a close if informal relationship with the Community.

Like all Jewish institutions it suffered under Nazi rule. After 1938, the hospital was no longer allowed to treat non-Jewish patients. After 1941, it was used by the Nazis as an assembly point for deportations. Most of the patients and staff were deported in February 1943, though the hospital, in extremely straitened circumstances, remained open throughout the Third Reich.

Today the Jewish Hospital enjoys particular repute in surgery and internal medicine, and serves as a teaching hospital connected to Humboldt University. In the foyer, there is an exhibition (in German) on the history of the hospital.

Jeanette-Wolff-Heim, Jüdisches Senioren-Zentrum
(Jeanette Wolff Senior Citizens' Home and the Jewish Senior Citizens' Center)
Dernburgerstrasse 36 (tel: 321 2056).
This home offers 67 private apartments, as well as a cafeteria, library, hair salon, and other appropriate facilities for Jewish senior citizens. The Center provides a wide range of activities, from Yoga classes to Torah discussion groups to field trips. It is named for Jeanette Wolff, a Holocaust survivor who returned to Berlin and served on the Berlin City Council and in the Bundestag.

Leo-Baeck-Altenwohnheim
(Leo Baeck Old Age Home)
Hebartstrasse 26 (tel: 321 2056).
This complex offers 72 private rooms with communal living and dining space in a Jewish environment. The kitchen is kosher and the

building contains a synagogue where regular Sabbath services are conducted. The building is next to the Jeanette Wolf Senior Citizens' Home and the two homes share many facilities and activities.

Treffpunkt Oranienburger Strasse
(Oranienburger Strasse Meeting Place)
Oranienburger Strasse 31 (tel: 282 3617).
An educational and activity center originally tailored for Russian immigrants, the *Treffpunkt* has proved popular with German-speakers as well. The *Treffpunkt* consists of a variety of classes, events and groups that use space in the Community offices on Oranienburger Strasse. Activities range from folkdancing classes to computer instruction to discussion groups on Jewish themes.

Zentralwohlfahrtstelle der Juden in Deutschland
(Central Welfare Office of Jews in Germany)
Oranienburger Str. 31 (tel: 282 6826).
Founded in 1917 and reorganized in 1951, this agency, composed of social workers and representatives from various local Jewish Communities and welfare organizations, deals with policy and budget issues on a national level.

GOVERNMENT SERVICES

Emigranten Programm
(Emigrants' Program)
Berliner Rathaus, Protokol 4C (tel: 2401 2610).
The Berlin administration has for many years conducted a program that brings Jewish Berliners forced to emigrate during the Nazi persecutions back for visits to the city. Participants are bussed about to get reacquainted with the city and visit places of interest. Some 30,000 people have participated thus far in the program.

JÜDISCHE VOLKSHOCHSCHULE

The Jüdische Volkshochschule—Jewish Adult Education Program—founded in 1962, is a unique institution in Germany. Each year, in three semesters, the full spectrum of Judaism is covered in over 50 lectures, readings, round-table discussions, concerts and more, often featuring well-known personalities. The Volkshochschule also sponsors special events that draw hundreds of visitors. In addition there's language instruction (Yiddish, Hebrew) as well as seminars with religious and cultural themes. Students include Jews as well as non-Jews. Since 1995, it has featured the only Jewish Film Festival in Germany.

Detailed schedules are available at the beginning of January, May, and October in the Jewish Community Center and Community offices at Oranienburger Strasse 29, as well as in selected cultural institutions and cafés. Schedules can also be requested by mail (just drop us a postcard).

Jüdische Volkshochschule
Jüdisches Gemeindehaus, Fasanenstrasse 79-80, 10623 Berlin
and Oranienburger Strasse 29, 10117 Berlin
Telephone: 88028-263, Fax: 88028-288
Office hours: Mon–Thu 1pm–4pm.

6 | Cemeteries

Melancholy, haunting, somber and inspiring, the Jewish cemeteries of Berlin evoke many, sometimes contradictory, responses. Even more so than the city's museums or monuments, the graveyards deliver a palpable sense of the Jewish experience in Berlin. Here the evolution, achievements and catastrophic fate of a once dynamic community are visible. Walking among the graves is a lesson in history and in memory.

A visit to one or more of these grave-yards, particularly the tree-shaded and often overgrown grounds of the Schön-hauser Allee and Weisensee cemeteries (the latter is the largest extant Jewish cemetery in Europe), is a special experience and highly recommended.

Men are expected to cover their heads; yarmulkes are available in the cemetery offices on the grounds.

■ Finding & Restoring Gravesites

A registry of all burials in the Weissen-see Cemetery has been preserved and is available for perusal in the cemetery office. Each entry notes the date of birth, date of death, and the location of the grave of the deceased. An in-complete list of the burials in the Schönhauser Allee Cemetery is also available. It is possible as well to arrange for the restoration of individual grave-stones and plots, though it does not necessarily come cheap. Call the Weissensee Cemetery Office at 925 3330 for more details.

Spandau-Kiewer
(The Spandau Gravestones)

Spandau Zitadelle, Am Juliusturm. **Transportation:** *U-Bahn line U7 to Spandau Zitadelle;* **Open:** *By appointment only. Call 334 6270 to schedule a viewing.*

The Spandau-Kiewer (from the Hebrew kever, "grave") is not a cemetery but a collection of medieval Jewish gravestones now on display in the Spandau Zitadelle (Spandau Citadel).

In 1955, during reconstruction work on the medieval Zitadelle, several gravestones with Hebrew inscriptions were discovered in the foundation walls. Eventually 65 stones and five fragments, dating from 1244 to 1474, were uncovered. As a result of their use as building material during the original construction of the fortress over four hundred years before, they remain remarkably well-pre-served. The source of these gravestones is uncertain, and it is pos-sible that they come from several different cemeteries. It has been suggested that there existed in Spandau in the thirteenth and four-teenth centuries a cemetery shared by the Spandau and Berlin Jewish communities that was broken up during the pogrom of 1349, as well as a second fifteenth-century graveyard destroyed after the expulsion of the Jews from the province in 1510. It was evidently after this second expulsion that the stones were uprooted for use in construction of the Zitadelle. A third fifteenth-century cemetery used by the Berlin community may also have been a source.

The oldest stone, from 1244, is that of Jona, son of Dan. (The first documentary evidence of the town of Berlin dates from this same year.) A particularly interesting stone is that of Eli'ezer, son of Moshe. It notes that he died as one of "ha'kodosh"—the holy—pro-bably meaning as a martyr, in 1347. The likelihood of an unnatural death is reinforced by the fact that the stone lists not his date of death, but that of his interment, the ninth of Av, a traditional day of mourning.

Several stones from the find can also be seen in the Jewish ceme-tery in Heerstrasse.

Friedhof Grosse Hamburger Strasse
(Grosse Hamburger Street Cemetery)

Grosse Hamburger Strasse 26. **Transportation:** *U-Bahn line U8 to Wein-meisterstrasse or S-Bahn line S3, S5, S7, or S9 to Hackescher Markt.*

This is the site of the first cemetery of Berlin's modern Jewish com-munity, dedicated in 1672 and closed in 1827. Destroyed by the Nazis in 1943, it is now a carefully groomed park that gives little sign that it was once an ivy-tangled, tree-shaded cemetery of over 12,000 graves. The single stone now standing—a replacement erected after the war—marks the resting place of the great Enlightenment philosopher Moses Mendelssohn. For a full description, see p. 119.

Friedhof Schönhauser Allee
(Schönhauser Allee Cemetery)

Schönhauser Allee 23-25. **Transportation:** *U-Bahn line U2 to Senefelder-platz;* **Open:** *Monday–Thursday 10am–4pm; Friday 10am–1pm.*

Although a law of 1794 forbid further interments within the city limits, it took another 30 years before the Jewish community was able to find and open a new cemetery here in keeping with the regu-lation. This 12 1/2 acre site was opened in 1827 and contains some 22,500 remains. Although it was officially closed in 1880, burials con-

Schönhauser Allee cemetery

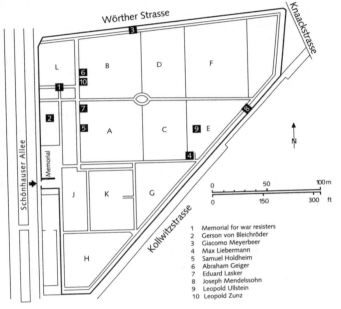

1 Memorial for war resisters
2 Gerson von Bleichröder
3 Giacomo Meyerbeer
4 Max Liebermann
5 Samuel Holdheim
6 Abraham Geiger
7 Eduard Lasker
8 Joseph Mendelssohn
9 Leopold Ullstein
10 Leopold Zunz

tinued as late as the 1970s.

Outside the cemetery, on the wall to the left of the entrance, is a plaque that reads: "This Jewish cemetery was dedicated in 1827. In the years from 1933–1945 it was destroyed by the Fascists. It should be preserved by posterity as an admonition."

Although the cemetery was severely damaged, it was not, like the Grosser Hamburger Strasse cemetery, obliterated. The Nazis stole much of the bronze and cast-iron work and, in early 1945, dug up many tombstones to erect a tank barrier in the street outside. There was additional damage from Allied bombs and mortars.

The condition of the graveyard now is the result of much renovation work. The quiet, leafy grounds and the many impressive and elegant old stones and tombs, ranging in style from Neoclassical to Art Nouveau, make a visit worthwhile.

To your left, as you enter the grounds, is a memorial wall with the inscription, "Here you stand silently, but when you turn away, do not remain silent."

About 250 feet down the main path to your left is an unusual memorial. A plaque attached to a small, fenced well reads: "Not to want the death of others was their death. At the end of 1944, war resisters hid here. They were discovered by the SS, hanged from the trees and tossed in here."

Notable figures buried in the graveyard include:

Gerson von Bleichröder (1822–93), who developed his father's banking company into one of the leading firms in Germany and became financial advisor to the "Iron Chancellor," Bismarck. In 1872 he was raised to the nobility. During the Congress of Berlin in 1878 he successfully prodded Bismarck to lobby for the emancipation of Romanian Jewry.

Giacomo Meyerbeer (1791–1864), whose given name was Jacob Liebmann Beer, was a composer of popular operas in the nineteenth century. Between 1818 and 1824 he worked in Italy, where he adopted an Italian name and received acclaim for several Italian operas. He later repeated his success in Paris with a number of French operas, including his most famous work, *Les Huguenots*. He was royal director of the opera in Berlin from 1842 to 1847, a rare state post for an unconverted Jew. His parents, **Jacob** and **Amalia Beer,** buried here as well, were prominent members of Berlin's Jewish community. In their home, the first Reform services in Berlin were held.

The painter **Max Liebermann** (1847–1935) was one of the foremost artists of his time. During his life he was considered the greatest of German Impressionists. His early paintings of working-class life and everyday scenes were at the time considered daring, though in his later years his paintings became staid. In 1898 he helped to found *Sezession* (Secession), an influential association of progressive artists. In 1920 he became president of the prestigious Berlin Academy of Art, a post he held until 1933, when he was ousted by the Nazis and his paintings were removed from all German museums. In 1943 his widow committed suicide to avoid imminent deportation by the Gestapo.

Abraham Geiger (1810–74) was one of the founders of the "Science of Judaism," an important modernizing movement that sought to reform Judaism by placing its beliefs and practices in historical context. In addition to being a prolific writer, he was a founder and director of the College for the Science of Judaism, which became an important center for reform studies.

Eduard Lasker (1829–84) was a prominent public figure and liberal politician. He was elected to the Prussian parliament and initially supported Bismarck in his drive for unification of the German states under Prussian leadership. Later he broke with Bismarck and founded the opposition Liberal Union Party. He was a staunch champion of Jewish rights. He died in New York while on a speaking tour.

Joseph Mendelssohn (1770–1848) eldest son of Moses, was the founder, with his younger brother Abraham (father of composer Felix Mendelssohn) of one of the country's most prestigious banking firms. Bankhaus Mendelssohn carried out a great deal of government business, including railway issues, state loans, and the transfer of French indemnities after Napoleon III's defeat. He also wrote a biography of his father Moses and was an active community leader. The bank was "Aryanized" during the Third Reich.

Leopold Ullstein (1829–99) was a prominent publisher and founder of one of the largest newspaper and book firms in the world. Starting out as a paper wholesaler, Ullstein eventually built an empire that published five daily newspapers, eight weekly papers, and myriad technical and literary books. The company was compulsorily sold to a Nazi firm in 1934 for six million marks, a tenth of its value.

The historian **Leopold Zunz** (1794–1886) was, along with Abraham Geiger, one of the founders of the "Science of Judaism" movement and one of the foremost scholars of Jewish history. He fought tirelessly for Jewish education, reform, and emancipation.

Friedhof Weissensee
(Weissensee Cemetery)

Herbert-Baum-Strasse 45 (tel: 925 3330). **Transportation:** *Tram 2, 3, 4, 13, 23, or 24 to Antonplatz; or S-Bahn line S8 or S10 to Greifswalder Strasse, then Tram 2, 3, or 4 two stops to Antonplatz;* **Open:** *Sunday–Thursday 7am–5pm (4pm in winter); Friday 7am–3pm.*

The last quarter of the nineteenth century was a golden age for Berlin Jewry; fully emancipated, they were—seemingly—completely integrated into the economic, political, and cultural life of the city. In addition, the German capital was a leading center of Jewish scholarship and philosophy and home to the most prestigious academies of both the Reform and Orthodox movements. Almost a third of Germany's Jews lived here.

The overgrown, ivy-shrouded Weissensee Cemetery is Europe's largest Jewish Cemetery.

The Weissensee Cemetery, opened in 1880, reflects this sense of accomplishment and strength. It is, at over 100 acres, the largest Jewish cemetery in Europe. As in Christian cemeteries of the time, tombs are often massive, elaborate affairs, an attempt to maintain status even after death. The cemetery features an imposing entrance portal and arcaded complex of yellow brick in Italian renaissance style that effectively conveys the community's pride.

Throughout the years of the Third Reich the cemetery was neglected and abused. During World War II, it sustained significant damage—a mortuary building was obliterated and some 4,000 graves damaged or destroyed. By the close of the war, the grounds were in complete disarray.

The first service to be held in Berlin after the war—and the first opportunity in many years for Jews to worship openly—was held here on May 11, 1945, in the main hall. Renovation work soon began but proceeded slowly: East Berlin contained a minuscule Jewish community and the government had little interest in the cemetery. Maintenance has improved since reunification as more money has become available. The fields near the entrance, particularly, have been cleared and are well-tended; farther back, toward the rear of the grounds, upkeep is less evident, and ivy and brush overrun the gravestones and mausoleums in a tangle of melancholy neglect.

In the forecourt a memorial tablet is encircled by stones engraved with the names of the major concentration camps. The inscription on the tablet reads "Remember eternally what happened to us. Dedicated to the memory of our murdered brothers and sisters 1933–1945 and to the living, that they fulfill the legacy of the dead." The two letters mounted on either side of the memorial tablet document the interment here of earth and ashes from Auschwitz on January 27, 1992, the 47th anniversary of the liberation of the camp.

The main path—the row of honor—begins to the right of the arcade. Here you'll find the graves of several lights of the community:

Louis Lewandowski (1821–94) was one of the nineteenth century's most significant composers of synagogue music. In 1866, he was appointed musical director of the New Synagogue and there helped to create music to accompany the liturgical changes of the new Reform movement. Many of his melodies and arrangements crossed the Atlantic and remain popular in the United States.

Hermann Cohen (1842–1918) was a prominent philosopher and the founder of the influential Marburg School of Neo-Kantianism. He left the University of Marburg in 1912 and came to Berlin to lecture on philosophy and Jewish theology. He believed in a Liberal Judaism that stressed ethics as opposed to the Orthodox emphasis on ritual and the Zionist stress on nationality.

Weissensee cemetery

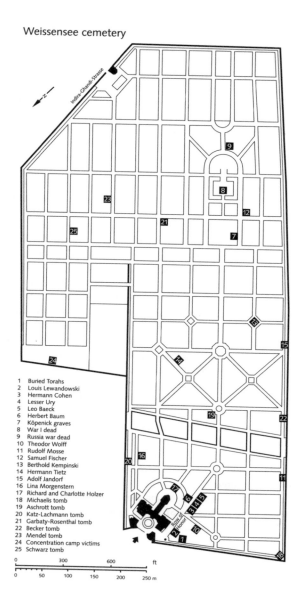

1   Buried Torahs
2   Louis Lewandowski
3   Hermann Cohen
4   Lesser Ury
5   Leo Baeck
6   Herbert Baum
7   Köpenick graves
8   War I dead
9   Russia war dead
10 Theodor Wolff
11 Rudolf Mosse
12 Samuel Fischer
13 Berthold Kempinski
14 Hermann Tietz
15 Adolf Jandorf
16 Lina Morgenstern
17 Richard and Charlotte Holzer
18 Michaelis tomb
19 Aschrott tomb
20 Katz-Lachmann tomb
21 Garbaty-Rosenthal tomb
22 Becker tomb
23 Mendel tomb
24 Concentration camp victims
25 Schwarz tomb

Lesser Ury (1861–1931) was a painter and graphic artist whose works form an important link between Impressionism and Expressionism. He lived in poverty until the age of 60, when his paintings —the most famous are melancholy nighttime cityscapes of wet pavements and gas lamps—finally achieved some popularity and began to sell. His works were banned by the Nazis and removed from all museums.

Leo Baeck (1873–1956) is buried in London, but his wife Natalie is buried here and his work is remembered on her stone. Philosopher, rabbi and writer, Baeck was one of the leading Jewish religious thinkers of the twentieth century. As president of the *Reichsvertretung*, the representative body of German Jews, he fought against the accelerating restrictions and persecutions of the early Nazi years. In 1933, soon after Hitler's appointment as Chancellor, he presciently declared that "the thousand-year history of German Jewry is at an end." Still, he refused to emigrate, and his principled conduct during his incarceration in Theresienstadt won him much admiration. In July 1945, he went to London, where he became president of the Council of Jews from Germany and Chairman of the World Union for Progressive Judaism.

On your left as you walk down the row of honor is a memorial to **Herbert Baum** (1912–42). He founded a communist resistance group, made up almost exclusively of young Jews, that was active as early as 1933. On May 18, 1942, his group set fire to an anti-Soviet and anti-Semitic Nazi propaganda exhibition, ironically entitled "The Soviet Paradise." The group was quickly rounded up by the Gestapo. He died on June 11, 1942, either as the result of torture or by his own hand to avoid further torture. On the back of his memorial are listed other members of the resistance group who were executed. The inscription reads: "They fell in struggles for peace and freedom."

Continuing along the main path for about three hundred yards, you'll see a large grassy mound. This is the site of the cemetery's second funeral home, which was destroyed by bombing in 1944. On the right-hand slope of the mound are 15 tombstones taken from a no-longer-extant Jewish graveyard in Köpenick, a southeastern suburb of Berlin that was once a separate municipality.

Beyond this mound is a walled field, laid out in 1926, for Jewish soldiers killed in action during World War I. The memorial, placed on an elevated terrace and resembling an alter, says "To the sons of the Jewish Community of Berlin killed in the World War." During World War I, Jews came under attack by right-wing nationalists for supposedly shirking their patriotic soldierly duties. (The charge was a staple of Nazi propaganda.) The stateliness of this special field of honor is, in part, a proud but defensive reaction by Berlin's Jews to this affront.

Behind the field, outside the wall, is another memorial to casualties of World War I, this one for Russian Jewish soldiers. The striking, Bauhaus-style marker reads "Here lie Russian soldiers who died in prison camps during the World War."

Many notable people have found a resting place in the Weissensee cemetery:

Theodor Wolff (1868–1943) was a journalist, author and the editor-in-chief of the *Berliner Tageblatt* newspaper. He was famous as the author of the paper's very popular Monday evening editorials. In 1918, he helped to found the liberal German Democratic Party. He fled to France on the night of the Reichstag fire, February 27, 1933, and died there in a concentration camp.

Rudolf Mosse (1843–1920) founded the Mosse publishing house in 1867. The firm was associated with several leading newspapers, including the *Berliner Tageblatt*, the *Deutsches Montagsblatt*, and the *Allgemeine Zeitung des Judentums*. He was also prominent as a philanthropist and activist in the Jewish community.

Samuel Fischer (1859–1934) was one of Germany's most respected publishers. Starting out as a bookseller, he founded *Fischer Verlag* in 1886 and his company soon became one of the country's leading literary publishers. Its authors included Thomas Mann, Arthur Schnitzler, and Sigmund Freud. The firm was forced out of Germany in 1936, but resumed publishing in the country in 1950 and is today again a respected name in publishing.

Berthold Kempinski (1845–1910) was a famous wine dealer and restaurateur whose restaurant, founded in 1873, became a prominent Berlin landmark and flourished until the Nazis came to power. The firm was "Aryanized" in 1937.

Hermann Tietz (1837–1907) was the co-founder, with his nephew **Oskar Tietz** (1858–1923), of the Hermann Tietz department stores, one of the most successful pre-war retail chains. The company eventually bought out *Kaufhaus Des Westens (KaDeWe)*, the huge store founded by **Adolf Jandorf** (1870–1932), who is also buried in this cemetery. The Hermann Tietz company was Aryanized by the

Nazis and the name shortened to *Hertie*, the monicker under which it still does business.

Lina Morgenstern (1830–1909) was an educational theorist and feminist. In 1873 she founded the *Berliner Hausfrauenverein* (Berlin Housewives' Association), which offered courses and lectures and lobbied for homemakers' welfare. She was also instrumental in convening the first International Women's Congress in Berlin in 1896.

Richard (1911–75) and **Charlotte** (1909–80) **Holzer** were members of the resistance group headed by Herbert Baum. They survived the war and were responsible for much of our knowledge about the activities of this group.

The graveyard is full of interesting, sometimes even outlandish tombstones and mausoleums. Particularly noteworthy efforts include:

The **Michaelis** tomb, a huge Italian renaissance cupola supported by sixteen Corinthian columns.

The **Aschrott** tomb, a massive red granite mausoleum with an Egyptian flavor.

The **Katz-Lachmann** tomb, a large Romanesque structure from unfinished stone featuring a vaulted roof and a round window.

The **Garbarty-Rosenthal** tomb, a triangular, neoclassical monument with paired Doric columns and enclosing wings. Josef Garbarty-Rosenthal (1851–1939) founded a prominent cigarette company that was Aryanized during the Nazi dictatorship.

The **Moritz Becker** (1830–1901) tomb features a stringently geometric design by Martin Dülfer which, though built just after the turn of the century, seems to anticipate Art Deco styling.

The merchant **Albert Mendel's** (1866–1922) gravestone was designed by Walter Gropius, the noted Bauhaus architect.

There are two other locations of special note:

By the northeast corner of the grounds is a section reserved for concentration camp victims. Interred here are several hundred urns, which, during the war and shortly thereafter, were mailed by surviving relatives to the cemetery for burial.

The mausoleum of the famous opera singer **Joseph Schwarz** (1880–1926) is an imposing structure that, with Doric columns and triangular pediment, resembles a Greek temple. It was used during the Third Reich by Jews in hiding as a safe refuge. In the middle of the ceiling is a glass plate that, when moved aside, was used to enter the small space under the roof, which served as a protected spot for rendezvous and sleeping. Underneath, an unintentionally appropriate line from Psalm 90 is inscribed on the tomb: "O Lord, you have been our refuge in every generation."

Friedhof Adass Jisroel
(Adass Yisroel Cemetery)

Wittlicher Strasse 2 (tel: 925 1724). **Transportation:** *Tram 2 or 18 to Falkenberger Strasse/Berliner Allee; Bus 155 or 158 to Piesporter Strasse or 255 or 259 to Berliner Allee/Rennbahnstrasse;* **Open:** *By appointment only. Call the Adass Yisroel office at 281 3135 to schedule a visit.*

The increasing liberality of Berlin's single, state-sanctioned congregation in the nineteenth century caused some Orthodox members to break away in 1869 and organize the Adass Yisroel congregation. Nine years later they purchased this plot in Weissensee. The small cemetery, just over five acres and containing about 3,000 plots, was only slightly damaged during the war, although the main building was destroyed by a bomb. After nearly half a century of neglect, the cemetery was renovated in 1985 by the newly reconstituted Adass Yisroel congregation.

A memorial stone by the entrance reads: "To the eternal memory of the members of the Israelite Synagogue Community (Adass Yisroel) of Berlin murdered by the Nazis."

Notable people interred here include:

Esriel Hildesheimer (1820–99), the first rabbi of the Adass Yisroel congregation and a founder, along with Samson Raphael Hirsch, of the neo-Orthodox movement, which attempted to accomodate western culture while maintaining strict orthodoxy. Acknowledged throughout the European Orthodox community as a leading scholar, he established the Rabbinical Seminary of Berlin, the country's first rabbinical school to combine orthodoxy with a secular academic curriculum, a controversial arrangement at the time.

David Hoffman (1843–1921) was the rector of the Adass Yisroel rabbinic seminary after Hildesheimer's death. He was also one of Europe's foremost Talmudic and Midrashic scholars.

Siegmund Breitbart (1893–1925) was a famous athlete and vaudeville performer known as the strongest man in Germany and nicknamed "the Iron King." He was acclaimed for such feats as bending iron bars and pulling trains by his teeth, but, somewhat ironically, died of blood poisoning from the scratch of a rusty nail.

Also worth a look are the gravestones of the **Schocken** family.

A. Only

Even before German reunification, the Orthodox Adass Yisroel congregation reestablished itself in east Berlin and renovated its cemetery.

These three stark white steles were designed by the expressionist architect Erich Mendelsohn.

Friedhof Heerstrasse
(Heerstrasse Cemetery)

Heerstrasse 141 (tel: 304 3234). ***Transportation:*** *Bus 149 to Scholzplatz.*
Open: *Sunday–Thursday 7am–5pm (in winter at 4pm. Friday 7am–3pm).*
The division of Berlin in 1948 also cleaved the Jewish community into eastern and western halves and stranded the Jewish cemetery

in Weissensee in the eastern Soviet sector. This necessitated the establishment of a Jewish cemetery for the community in the west. This well-groomed plot, tucked away in woodlands on the western outskirts of the city, was consecrated in 1955 and now contains about 4,500 graves.

The first tombstone you'll encounter on the main path marks the grave of **Heinz Galinski** (1912–1992), the longtime post-war chairman of the Jewish Community of Berlin and later of the Central Council of Jews in Germany. Next to his marker, several of the medieval gravestones uncovered in Spandau are set, drawing attention to the long history and continuity of the Jewish community in Germany.

At the end of the path is a small memorial dedicated to the victims of the Holocaust: The inscription on the stone, referring to Hitler, states, "To the eternal memory of those that had to lose their lives under the domination of the monster, 1933–1945." In front of the stone, ashes from Auschwitz have been interred. Behind it are markers for individuals and families murdered in the camps.

Prominent people buried here include:

Ernst Deutsch (1890–1969), one of the most famous German actors of his time. He worked a great deal with Max Reinhardt and played in the famous 1920 silent film "The Golem." With the rise of Hitler he left Germany and worked in London and Hollywood.

Hans Rosenthal (1925–87), a famous radio and television moderator and executive in postwar Germany. He lost his parents and brother to the Nazis and lived underground in Berlin for the last two years of the war. After liberation, he began a career in radio and switched to television in 1967, where he had great success with a quiz show called "Dalli-Dalli." In addition, he was a member of the Central Council of Jews in Germany and a representative of the Berlin Community Board.

Jeanette Wolff (1888–1976) survived twelve years in concentration camps and after the war became a representative for the Social Democratic Party in the Berlin City Council and the Bundestag. She also served as chair of the Jewish Community Board and Central Welfare Office.

There are several prominent Jews and Christians of Jewish descent buried elsewhere in the city. These include:

**Friedhöfe der Jerusalems und Neuen Kirchengemeinde
(Jerusalem and New Churches Community Cemeteries)**
*Mehringdamm 21 (tel: 622 1063). **Transportation:** U Bahn line U1 or U6 to
Hallesches Tor or U6 or U7 to Mehringdamm; **Open:** Daily, summertime:
8am–6pm, wintertime: 8am–4pm.*

Felix Mendelssohn (1809–47) was a world-renowned composer, pianist and conductor. In addition to his writing, playing, and conducting work, he was the foremost musical authority of his day, a mentor to Schumann, Chopin, and other composers, and the initiator of the revival of the music of J.S. Bach. His work includes *The Scottish Symphony, The Italian Symphony, Violin Concerto in E minor,* and incidental music to *A Midsummer Night's Dream,* which includes his famous *Wedding March.* His gravestone is inscribed with his full name, Jacob Ludwig Felix Mendelssohn Bartholdy.

His sister **Fanny Hensel** (1805–47), a talented composer in her own right, is buried beside him. His parents, **Abraham Mendelssohn Bartholdy** (1776–1835) second son of Moses Mendelssohn, and his wife **Lea** (1778–1842) are buried in a fenced plot behind their children. It was Abraham who, motivated by practical rather than religious considerations, had his children baptized in 1816 and followed suit with his wife in 1822. He added the name Bartholdy, which came from a piece of property that Lea's brother owned, because, as he once remarked, "a Christian Mendelssohn is an impossibility."

In the same field about twenty yards to the east is the grave of **Rahel Varnhagen** (1771–1833). She was the most famous and popular hostess during Berlin's celebrated salon age. Berlin's salons, almost all of which were organized by Jewish society women, were the artistic and literary centers of the city in the late eighteenth and early nineteenth century. Visitors to her distinguished gatherings included Heinrich Heine, Wilhelm and Alexander von Humboldt and the writer Karl August Varnhagen von Ense, whom she married in 1814. She converted to Protestantism just four days before their wedding.

In the next field to the east lies **Henrietta Herz** (1764–1847), who founded the first of Berlin's famous salons around 1779, just after she married Marcus Herz, one of Berlin's most prominent Jewish intellectuals, at the tender age of 15. Her wit and her beauty made the Herz home a popular gathering place for Berlin's society of arts and letters. Marcus Herz died in 1803. Henrietta converted to Protestantism in 1817.

Dorotheenstädtischer Friedhof
(Dorotheenstaedtischen Cemetery)

Chauseestr. 126 (tel: 461 7279). ***Transportation:*** *U-Bahn line U6 to Oranienburger Tor; Tram 1 or 13 to Oranienburger Tor; Bus 157 to Schlegelstrasse;* ***Open:*** *Daily, summertime: 8am–6pm, wintertime 8am–5pm.*

This cemetery was even in the eighteenth century a favorite for prominent people. After the war, it served in the (officially atheist) communist state as a non-denominational resting place for many prominent figures, several of them Jewish:

Paul Dessau (1894–1979), the grandson of a cantor, achieved recognition for his compositions in the 1920s, but only found his mature style after meeting playwright Bertolt Brecht in 1942, when both were refugees in the United States. His most popular works include the music to Brecht's *The Judgment of Lucullus* and the opera *Einstein*.

Hanns Eisler (1898–1962) was also a composer who worked with Brecht. A student of Schoenberg and Anton von Webern, he emigrated to the United States in 1937. For many years he composed movie scores in Hollywood and served as a musical assistant to Charlie Chaplin, but his left-wing politics eventually resulted in a session before the House Committee on un-American Activities and his deportation. He settled in East Berlin in 1948 and continued his collaborations with Brecht, which included the German Democratic Republic's national anthem, *Solidaritätslied* (Solidarity Song).

John Heartfield (1891–1968) is famous for his photo montages from the 1920s and '30s, many of which were directed against the Nazis. Born Helmut Herzfeld, he anglicized his name to protest anti-British war hysteria and chauvinism during World War I.

Helene Weigel (1900–71) was an actress married to Bertolt Brecht. She led the Berliner Ensemble theater group, East Germany's most important, after Brecht's death. She converted to Protestantism in 1928.

Arnold Zweig (1887–1968) was a novelist and playwright and editor for a time of the Zionist *Jüdische Rundschau* newspaper. When the Nazis came to power, he moved to Palestine. He later grew critical of Zionism and, turning toward communism, resettled in East Berlin.

Anna Seghers (1900–83), born Netty Reiling, was a popular novelist and writer particularly feted in East Germany for her radical politics. Forced to flee the country in 1933, she returned to Berlin in 1947. Her most famous work is *The Seventh Cross*.

7 | Museums

Berlin has a number of museums of great renown. Yet the city has long had trouble with a Jewish museum. The first, opened in 1933, was closed by the Nazis five years later. The current Jewish Museum, for many years relegated to inadequate temporary rooms and just now finding a permanent home, has been beset by controversy and squabbles for several years. Politicians, bureaucrats, curators, and the Jewish Community have squabbled over such questions as whether the museum will be an independent entity or a department of the city-run Berlin Museum; whether it will have a separate budget or be included in the funding for the larger museum; whether the Jewish Community will have a substantive role or not, and more.

Things got so unruly that an outsider was brought in to serve as interim director and peacemaker: Michael Blumenthal, who has enjoyed a long career in public service, most notably as President Carter's Secretary of the Treasury. He has mapped out a plan that gives the museum a degree of autonomy by creating a seperate foundation for it. Whether this will ultimately satisfy all sides remains to be seen.

In the meantime, several Berlin museums boast excellent exhibitions of Jewish interest. For temporary exhibitions, check out one of the city program magazines (*Zitty*, *Tip*, or *Berlin Programm*). Several of the places listed in the "Third Reich Sites" chapter also feature relevent exhibitions.

■ Patrons of the Arts

As collectors, donors, and benefactors, Jews played a part in the development of many of Berlin's museums in the nineteenth and early twentieth centuries. The most notable was the industrialist and art collector James Simon, who donated extensive collections to the Kaiser Wilhelm (now the Bode) Museum and the Museum für Volkskunde (Museum of Ethnology). He also financed the expedition that uncovered the famous bust of Egyptian Queen Nefertiti and then gave the regal head to the Egyptian Museum. A bust of Simon is now displayed in the lobby of the museum. This tradition has been carried on by Heinz Berggruen, a native Berliner who, after fleeing the city in 1938, became an art dealer in Paris and a friend of Picasso. Over a half century later, he donated a collection of 90 artworks by Picasso, Klee, and others to the city, which installed them in November, 1996, in their own museum in the Stülerbau across the street from Charlottenburg Palace.

Jüdisches Museum Berlin
(Jewish Museum Berlin)

Lindenstrasse 14 (tel. 259 93410). **Transportation:** *U-Bahn line U1 or U6 to Hallesches Tor; Bus 240 to Am Berlin Museum. (Due to open in 2000).*

The most striking thing about the Jewish Museum is not its collection, but rather the building in which it is housed. The structure, by Daniel Libeskind, is an arresting post-modern building that attempts to depict architecturally the unsettling history presented inside.

The long, thin, angular structure cuts back and forth and out like an unsprung lightning bolt. It is clad in zinc and riven by an irregular arrangement of angular windows. Cutting straight through the various folds of the building is an empty shaft or corridor—what Libeskind calls a "voided void"—a structural metaphor for the absent Jewish element in Berlin life. It is a remarkable building, one sure to become a Berlin landmark.

Outside, the architect has designed the E.T.A. Hoffmann Garden, another striking design of stark, square pillars, tightly bundled and angled, meant to simulate the exile's experience of disorientation.

The museum's collection of Judaica is a strong but not especially notable one. Some of the items come from the city's original Jewish Museum, the private institution run by the Jewish Community until 1938.

A particularly interesting piece is a *parochet*—Torah curtain—dating from around 1750 that once hung in Berlin's first synagogue in Heidereutergasse. The synagogue was destroyed during the Kristallnacht pogrom. The *parochet* was concealed in a walled-up room until the defeat of Germany and was thereby saved.

Paintings and drawings include works by Jewish artists Daniel Oppenheim, Lesser Ury, Jacob Steinhardt, and Max Liebermann, among others. There are also works on Jewish themes by non-Jewish artists, a notable example being a portrait by Edvard Munch of the famous industrialist and public servant Walther Rathenau.

The museum and its exhibitions are still in the planning stages. Though there will be a permanent exhibit on the history of Jews in Germany, the specific content of it is at this time undecided. Before the museum's opening, the Libeskind building will be open for architectural tours, a good opportunity to see this landmark structure from the inside. Call the museum office for information.

Bitter Bredt

Daniel Libeskind's post-modern design promises to make the Jewish Museum a city landmark.

Stiftung Centrum Judaicum—Neue Synagoge Berlin
(Centrum Judaicum—New Synagogue Berlin Foundation)

*Oranienburger Strasse 30 (tel. 284 01250). **Transportation:** U-Bahn line U6 to Oranienburger Tor; S-Bahn line S1 or S2 to Oranienburger Strasse; Tram 1 or 13 to Oranienburger Strasse. **Open:** Sunday–Thursday 10am–6pm, Friday until 2pm, closed Saturday.*

The New Synagogue, built in 1866 and long a Berlin landmark, was damaged in the Kristallnacht pogrom and virtually destroyed by Allied bombing during the war. For nearly fifty years afterwards, it remained a ruin. In 1988 the Centrum Judaicum—New Synagogue Berlin Foundation was established to renovate the building and turn it into a museum, cultural center, and research facility.

Inside, the few details and structural elements that survived were preserved, but no attempt was made to replace missing pieces with period copies. You can see original elements throughout the building, but the effect is especially striking upstairs in the room once used by the Jewish Community's board of directors and in the lobby and vestibule on the ground floor.

The Foundation's permanent exhibit on the history and reconstruction of the synagogue begins in the lobby and moves on into the vestibule, where fragments of stained glass, pieces of iron decoration, remnants of the bima, and other objects unearthed during reconstruction are displayed like rare archeological finds. Here the synagogue's original Ner Tamid, unearthed almost intact in the renovation work's most exciting discovery, is displayed.

In the next room is a second exhibition, entitled "The New Synagogue and Jewish Life in Central Berlin" that presents the rich and varied Jewish presence in the neighborhood around the New Synagogue in the years just prior to the Nazi cataclysm. It includes both rare and everyday artifacts from religious congregations, social organizations, schools and other groups, institutions, and individuals that made up the strong fabric of Jewish life at the time. The exhibition also takes a look at the contemporary state of Jewish life in the neighborhood, a striking contrast, it goes without saying. Both exhibitions feature labels in English. The New Synagogue also regularly hosts temporary exhibitions, usually on aspects of Berlin Jewish history or culture.

Gedenkstätte Deutscher Widerstand
(The German Resistance Memorial Center)

Stauffenbergstrasse 13-14 (2654 2202). **Transportation:** *U-Bahn line U1 or U15 to Kurfürstenstrasse, then bus 148 or 348 to Potsdamer Brücke; Bus 129 to Gedenkstätte Deutscher Widerstand.* **Open:** *Monday–Friday 9am–6pm, Saturday, Sunday & Holidays 9am–1pm.*

In overwhelming and exhausting detail, the German Resistance Memorial Center documents domestic resistance to the National Socialists. In 26 rooms, various movements, methods, and groups are described. They range from the passive opposition of religious leaders, writers and intellectuals to active resistance organizations such as the White Rose student group, the Harnack/Schulze-Boysen Organization (sometimes called the Red Orchestra), and, in particular detail, the military conspiracy behind the July 20, 1944 attempt to assassinate Hitler.

The building that houses the museum, called the Bendler Block, was used before and during the war by the military for administrative purposes. The exhibit itself is housed on the third floor of the former Army headquarters, the floor which contained the office of Claus Schenk Graf von Stauffenberg. He was the young lieutenant-colonel who, as part of the July 20th conspiracy, placed the bomb in the conference room at Hitler's headquarters in the "Wolf's Lair," in Rastenburg, East Prussia. In the aftermath of the failed coup, the several dozen military officers involved were rounded up and executed. Stauffenberg and three others were summarily shot that night in the building's courtyard. This yard, which you will pass through on your way to the exhibition rooms, has been turned into a memorial.

One of the museum rooms is supposedly devoted to Jewish resistance, although much of it is given over to a familiar discussion of the persecution and destruction of the Jews during the Third Reich. There is, however, some consideration of self-help groups, cultural activities, and emigration in the context of resistance. Additionally, there are accounts of important resistance groups such as the *Gemeinschaft für Frieden und Aufbau* (Community for Peace and Reconstruction) and the *Chug Chaluzi* (Pioneer Circle) underground Zionists. For an account of the best-known German-Jewish resistance organization, the Herbert Baum Group, one must move on to another room—"Working Class Resistance after 1939"—as they are considered here to be primarily a communist organization.

All exhibits are in German, although a general pamphlet in English on the exhibition is available. The Memorial Center also offers information in English on the subject of Jewish resistance and non-Jewish resistance on behalf of Jews. Ask at the main desk.

Deutsches Historisches Museum
(German Historical Museum)

Unter den Linden 2 (tel: 203 040). **Transportation:** *U-Bahn line U6 to Französische Strasse; Buses 100, 157 or 348 to Deutsche Staatsoper.*
Open: *Daily except Wednesdays 10am–6pm.*

Housed in the Zeughaus, a former armory that is one of Berlin's few surviving Baroque buildings, the German Historical Museum is intended as the main German history museum in the new capital. Its principal exhibit chronicles the country's history from the Middle Ages to reunification through an impressive collection of paintings, documents, artifacts, and ephemera.

Tucked in among the 2,000 items are a handful that deal with German Jewry. The earliest piece is an illustrated broadsheet from

1484 entitled *Der Judenwucher* (The Jewish Usurer), a diatribe in Latin against Jewish lending practices. Other noteworthy pieces include a certificate of protection for *Schutzjude* (protected Jew) Abraham Meyer Jacob dating from 1755, a bust of Moses Mendelssohn, an 1834 portrait of Felix Mendelssohn, and a painting from 1842 entitled *Die Pfandleihe* (The Pawnbroker) that shows a couple of caricatured Jews taking advantage of peasants. It is not much different from the Latin manuscript written 350 years before.

Examples of political anti-Semitism crop up when the exhibition reaches the years of the Weimar Republic (1919–33). You can see, with mounting dread, the increasing level and sophistication of fascist propaganda—material which begins as the primitive rantings of extremists and ends as the mainstream of public opinion.

The Nazi years and the treatment of Jews under the Third Reich are illustrated with documents, posters, and other items, including an anti-Semitic children's book entitled *"Trau keinem Fuchs auf grüner Heid und keinem Jud bei seinem Eid!"* (Don't trust a fox on a green heath or a Yid on his oath), wall charts that graphically explain the Nuremberg Laws racial classifications, and other ephemera of the Thousand-Year Reich. There is also a small model of the selection ramp and gas chambers at Auschwitz.

A hefty catalog of the main exhibition is available in English and tours in English can be arranged by calling the office.

Ephraimpalais
(Ephraim Palace)

Poststrasse 16 (tel: 24 00 20). **Transportation:** *U-Bahn line U2 or U8 to Alexanderplatz; S-Bahn line S3, S5, S7, S9 or S75 to Alexanderplatz; Buses 142 or 257 to Mühlendamm Brücke.* **Open:** *Daily except Monday 10am–6pm.* This mansion, considered the finest example of Baroque architecture in the city when it was built, was the home of Veitel Heine Ephraim (1703–75), a banker and minter for King Frederick II and prominent member of the Jewish community. The original building was torn down in 1935, although parts of the facade were saved and incorporated in the new structure built in 1987.

The mansion is now a department of the Berlin Museum. It does not contain exhibits of particular Jewish content, although its art collection, displayed on the second floor, does feature a work by the Berlin Jewish painter Lesser Ury.

8 | Memorials

Berlin contains a tremendous number of memorials of Jewish interest; most of them, of course, address the persecution and destruction of the Jews during the years of Nazi rule. Scores of sculptures, stones, plaques, and artworks mark the locations of desecrated synagogues, points of deportation, the homes of expelled and murdered residents, sites of destruction, points of resistance, and the theme of the Holocaust in general.

This wealth of memorials is of relatively recent vintage. It is only in the last 10 or fifteen years that government and civic groups have developed much enthusiasm to remember, mourn and admonish. Prior to that time, there was, at least in the western sectors, an avoidance of the subject of the German destruction of the Jews. In the eastern half of the city, the persecution and destruction of the Jews were generally ignored in favor of plaques or sculptures to resistance fighters and communists.

Many Berlin Holocaust memorials are extremely didactic, presenting extensive historical discourses or long lists of names or numbers. Others display an almost furious attempt to attract attention and to spur remembrance. Over the years, the memorials have grown in size and ambition. One of the first Berlin memorials, erected in Steinplatz in 1953, is a modest stone marker, chest-high, with an inscription that reads "1933–1945—To the victims of National Socialism." The planned National Memorial to the Murdered Jews of Europe, in contrast, is slated to occupy an entire city block. Whether anything is gained by this enlargement is debatable.

■ Holocaust Memorial?

A proposal for a national "Memorial to the Murdered Jews of Europe," initiated several years ago and at first greeted with great enthusiasm, has lately come under increasing criticism and is years behind schedule. The winning design, chosen after five years, two competitions, and over 500 proposals, calls for a huge field of thousands of upright concrete slabs. Critics say it is too grandiose and inscrutable. Some say money should go instead to the surviving concentration camps. Others maintain that the crimes of the Holocaust cannot be evoked aethestically. Still others assert that there are simply too many memorials in Germany. Politicians are dragging their feet in approving the increasingly controversial project, and it is unclear at the moment whether the memorial will ever be built.

Memorials relevant to the Jewish experience in Berlin are included here; the many plaques, most of which note places of birth or residence of famous Jews, are not.

CHARLOTTENBURG

Treblinka

Amtsgerichtplatz (between Suarezstrasse and Holtzendorffstrasse); ***Transportation:*** *U-Bahn line U2 to Sophie-Charlotte-Platz; Bus 110, 149, 204 to Amtsgerichtplatz.*

This abstract bronze sculpture, its design suggestive of stacked human corpses, memorializes the over 700,000 Jews murdered in the death camp of Treblinka. The sculpture was created in 1966 by the Czech sculptor Vadim Sidur and placed here, in front of the Charlottenburg district court, in 1979.

Memorial Stone for the Victims of National Socialism

Steinplatz (Hardenbergstrasse between Uhlandstrasse and Goethe Strasse). ***Transportation:*** *U-Bahn line U2 or U9 or S-Bahn line S3, S5, S7, S9, or S75 to Zoologischer Garten; Bus 145 or 245 to Steinplatz.*

This simple marker—consisting of stone from the destroyed synagogue on Fasanenstrasse—was the first Berlin monument to Jews murdered during the Third Reich. It was erected in 1953, not by the state but by a private group, the Union of the Persecuted of the Nazi Regime, partially in response to the stone on the opposite corner of Steinplatz, which commemorates the victims of Stalinism and was put up two years earlier. The inscription reads: "1933–1945—To the victims of National Socialism."

Jewish Community Center Memorial Courtyard

Fasanenstrasse 79-80. ***Transportation:*** *U-Bahn line U2 or U9 or S-Bahn line S3, S5, S7, S9, or S75 to Zoologischer Garten; Bus 149 to Joachimstaler Strasse or Bus 109, 119, 129 or 219 to Uhlandstrasse.*

Situated within the Jewish Community Center, this small courtyard, featuring a wall with the names of the major concentration camps and ghettos, serves as a quiet spot for remembrance and contemplation. In a sense, it is Berlin's only "Jewish" memorial, created by the Community and intended, basically, for its own use. The Community's annual remembrance of the Kristallnacht pogrom takes place here.

Just before you enter the courtyard, you'll see a plaque for Recha Freier, with the inscription: "Founder of Youth Aliyah, Recha Freier, 1892–1984, who rescued uncounted Jewish children from extermination by the Nazi regime and brought them to Palestine. 'The saved become redeemers.'"

In response to increasing anti-Semitism in 1930s Germany, Recha Freier founded *Jugend Alijah* (Youth Aliyah) to prepare and facilitate emigration to Palestine for teenagers. By the end of 1939, the group had helped 4,788 young Jews to emigrate. In 1940 she traveled to Yugoslavia, where she saved 120 children by smuggling them over the Balkans to Palestine. She settled in Palestine in 1941.

On your left as you enter the courtyard is a plaque commemorating two famous Jewish tenors, Joseph Schmidt and Richard Tauber, whose success on stage, film and recordings was cut short when the Nazis assumed power. The plaque reads "Voices that will never die away—in remembrance of Joseph Schmidt (Mar. 6, 1904–Nov 16, 1942) Richard Tauber (May 16, 1892–Jan. 8, 1948). Dedicated on the occasion of the January 9, 1963 event for the 60th birthday of Herbert Zernik in the Jewish Commuity Center."

Next to it is a tablet from B'nai B'rith:

"In lasting memory of the former VIII German district, and its sisters and brothers led by the distinguished presidents Fenchel, Maratzki, Timendorfer and Baeck in everlasting thankfulness." On the adjoining wall is a relief portrait of Walther Rathenau that commemorates the former Foreign Minister, assassinated by right-wing nationalists in 1922. To the right of this tablet is one last plaque:

"In remembrance of the 60,000 Jewish citizens of Berlin. Heinrich Stahl and Dr. Otto Hirsch, representing the employees of the Jewish Community and Jewish organizations that in the years 1933–45 lost their lives during the National Socialist regime."

Heinrich Stahl was chairman of the board of directors of the Berlin Jewish Community under the Nazis. Sent to Theresienstadt in 1942, he served briefly as deputy chairman of the camp council (Judenrat) before his death the same year.

Otto Hirsch, a lawyer, served in several important government and Jewish Community posts before his election in 1933 as executive director of the newly organized *Reichsvertretung der deutschen Juden*, the first national organization of German Jews, set up to respond to the Nazi threat. Despite several offers from abroad, Hirsch refused to emigrate and was arrested and sent to Mauthausen concentration camp in 1941, where he was murdered.

Torah Sculpture

Fasanenstrasse 79-80 (outside the Jewish Community Center).
Transportation: *U-Bahn line U2 or U9 or S-Bahn line S3, S5, S7, S9, or S75 to Zoologischer Garten; Bus 149 to Joachimstaler Strasse or Bus 109, 119, 129 or 219 to Uhlandstrasse.*
A bronze Torah set in stone with the inscription "There shall be one law for you and for the resident stranger among you" (from Numbers 15:16). It was designed by Richard Hess and erected in 1987.

KREUZBERG

Carl Herz Memorial

Yorckstrasse 4-11 (in front of the Kreuzberg district city hall).
Transportation: *U-Bahn line U6 or U7 to Mehringdamm; Bus 119, 140, or 219 to Mehringdamm.*
This small sculpture, a rough-hewn head of bronze perched upon a column, commemorates the pre-Third Reich district president of Kreuzberg, Carl Herz. On March 10, 1933, his office was raided by the SA, who drove him into the street outside with a sign hanging from his neck that read "I am a Jewish swine." He was subsequently forced from office. Herz moved to London in 1939 and immigrated to Israel in 1946.

The text written on the column reads: "Carl Herz, born 1877 in Göthen, died 1951 in Haifa, was elected mayor of Kreuzberg for a term from 1926 until 1938. In 1933, the Nazis drove him out of city hall for political and 'racial' reasons. Because he worked tirelessly for the establishment of a democratic administration, Dr. Carl Herz, the respected jurist and outstanding Social Democrat, was one of the first local politicians to be removed from office by the new powerholders. 'The exceedingly great organizational, economic, and scientific powers of the German people must not be used for the destruction of the world, but for its improvement.' Dr. Carl Herz, Haifa, 1951." The sculpture was created in 1985 by Professor Joachim Dunkel and installed by the Kreuzberg district council.

Kottbusser Ufer Synagogue memorials

Fraenkelufer 10-16. **Transportation:** *U-Bahn line U1 or U8 to Kottbusser Tor;*

Bus 141 to Kottbusser Brücke.

Two plaques commemorate the synagogue that once stood here. The small memorial located to the east of the synagogue gate reads: "Here one of the two major synagogues in Kreuzberg was located. In the night of the pogrom, November 9th to 10th, 1938, the National Socialists burned down the synagogue. The damaged main building was torn down in 1958. The former youth and weekday synagogue was preserved and today serves as one of Berlin's Jewish Community centers." This memorial was created by Cornelia Lengfeld in 1988.

In 1995 an information plaque describing the history of the synagogue and its destruction was erected across the street. The long text, which provides some history of the building, reads as follows:

The Orthodox Synagogue on Kottbusser Ufer

(today: Fraenkelufer).

In the years 1913 to 1916, the Jewish Community built here one of Berlin's largest synagogues. It offered seating for 2000 people and served as a House of God for the traditional segment of the Community. That meant that services were celebrated according to a traditional liturgy, and not, as in the New Synagogue, with a mixed choir and organ accompaniment.The architect Alexander Beer designed a neo-classical building, mixed with other stylistic elements, in the form of a pillared basilica with three aisles, the facade of which faced the shore of the Landwehr canal. A special feature was the spacious entry hall behind a four-pillared portal. Until 1932, the rabbi was Isidor Bleichrode and the cantor was Arno Nadel, who was also well-known as a poet and painter, as well as a composer and collector of old Jewish songs. Next to the synagogue stood the community center, still standing to this day, which accomodated a weekday synagogue, a prayer room for youth services, administrative offices and, from 1925, a day care center. In 1935, in the cellar of the synagogue, the community built a relief kitchen. In the pogrom of November 9–10, 1938, the furnishings of the synagogue were largely devastated. Nazis and residents who joined the pogrom set fire to the interior, burned the Torahs and destroyed ritual objects. How badly the building itself was damaged is today impossible to establish. In any case, after the pogrom the community could no longer celebrate services in the main synagogue. In January 1942, the Gestapo confiscated the building, using it to store expropriated Jewish property before auctioning it off, and parking military vehicles there. The youth and weekday synagogue remained largely undamaged. From 1938 to 1942 Sabbath services, sometimes given in several consecutive seatings, were held there under very straitened circumstances. After the end of the war, the synagogue, almost completely destroyed by high-explosive bombs, was given back to the Jewish Community. Already by the Jewish New Year in September 1945, services took place again in the nearly undestroyed community center. Reconstruction was at that time contemplated neither by the city of Berlin nor the few returning community members who had survived the extermination camps or underground. In the late '50s, the ruins of the old main synagogue were pulled down and the surviving former youth synagogue renovated. To this day it is a synagogue of the Jewish Community of Berlin. In remembrance of November 9, 1938, the city council of Berlin delivered to the synagogue board of directors in 1968 a restored Torah curtain, which was found damaged but not completely destroyed during the clearing of the main synagogue. For the same reason, the Kreuzberg district council set up in November 1988 a memorial created by the sculptor Cornelia Lengfeld. It marks the place at which the southwest corner of the synagogue touched the streetline. Today the synagogue plot is a public park.

Memorial Stone for the Jewish Cultural Union Theater

Kommandentenstrasse 57. **Transportation:** *U-Bahn line U2 to Spittlemarkt; Bus 240 to Kommandantenstrasse.*

This simple granite marker, looking very much like a gravestone, commemorates the Jewish Cultural Union Theater, an organization that attempted to provide work and entertainment for Jews under the restrictions imposed by the Nazis. The inscription beneath provides the following explanation:

"Here the Jewish Cultural Union Theater was located from 1935–1941. Excluded from professional life, the Jews in Germany founded this self-help organization with its own orchestra and ensembles for opera, operetta, and theater. The Nazi authorities misused the Cultural Union for surveillance of Jewish artists and their audiences, which could consist only of Jews. In 1941, it was prohibited. Almost all of those who worked here were murdered in concentration camps." The memorial, installed in 1990, is by Susanne Ahner.

MITTE

Grosse Hamburger Strasse Memorial

Grosse Hamburger Strasse 26. **Transportation:** *U-Bahn line U8 to Weinmeisterstrasse or S-Bahn line S3, S5, S7, or S9 to Hackescher Markt.*

An dieser Stelle befand sich das erste Altenheim der Jüdischen Gemeinde Berlin. 1942 verwandelte die Gestapo es in ein Sammellager für jüdische Bürger.

55000 Berliner Juden vom Säugling bis zum Greis wurden in die KZ-Lager Auschwitz und Theresienstadt verschleppt und bestialisch ermordet.

VERGESST DAS NIE
WEHRET DEM KRIEG
HÜTET DEN FRIEDEN

A plaque now marks the site in Grosse Hamburger Strasse where Jews were incarcerated prior to being sent to Auschwitz and Theresienstadt.

This memorial was erected in 1985 to commemorate the 55,000 Jews who passed through this site—a Jewish old age home taken over by the Nazis and used as a prison and collection center—before deportation to Theresienstadt and Auschwitz. The 13 female figures are by Will Lammert, who also created the central memorial at Ravensbruck concentration camp. These figures were among 15 originally intended for Ravensbrück and left unfinished at Lammert's death in 1957. In 1985 they were cast and arranged especially for this memorial.

To the left of the figures is a memorial tablet that reads: "On this site stood the first old-age home of Berlin's Jewish community, transformed by the Gestapo in 1942 into a collection camp for Jewish citizens. 55,000 Berlin Jews from infants to the elderly were shipped to Auschwitz and Theresienstadt concentration camps and bestially murdered. Never forget it; prevent war; safeguard peace."

Denkmal für das Wirken jüdischer Bürger in Berlin
(Memorial to the Contributions of the Jewish Citizens in Berlin)
Koppenplatz. **Transportation:** *U-Bahn line U8 to Rosenthaler Platz or Weinmeisterstrasse; Bus 340 to Tucholskystrasse.*

In 1988, for the 50th anniversary of the Kristallnacht pogrom, the East German government called for a competition to commemorate the former Jewish residents of the area—the first large memorial dedicated in the German Democratic Republic to Berlin's Jews. The communist government expired before the memorial was built, and it was not until 1996, when the park grounds of Koppenplatz were redone, that the sculpture was finally installed.

The memorial, cast in bronze, is a wall-less representation of a room, consisting of only a parquet floor, a desk and two chairs. One chair lies knocked over on the floor, a symbol of abrupt, forced departure. Around the perimeter of the floor are these words, taken from a 1947 poem by the Jewish poet Nelly Sachs:

" 'Oh, the dwelling places of death,/Invitingly prepared/For the house's host, who was otherwise a guest-/Oh, you fingers,/The threshhold laying/Like a knife between life and death-//Oh, you chimneys,/Oh, you fingers,/and Israel's body through the air in smoke!' Nelly Sachs (December 10, 1891 Berlin – May 12, 1970 Stockholm)."

The stark sculpture, understated yet more eloquent than many of the other more effusive memorials in the city, is by Karl Biedermann.

Block der Frauen
(Block of Women)

Rosenstrasse 2-4. **Transportation:** *S-Bahn line S3, S5, S7, or S9 to Hackescher Markt; Bus 100, 157, or 348 to Spandauer Strasse.*

This sculpture, created by Ingeborg Hunzinger in 1995, commemorates the Rosenstrasse Women's Protest, the single known instance of mass public protest during the Nazi regime. Here several hundred Gentile women assembled to demand the release—successfully—of their Jewish husbands and children from a Gestapo detention center on Rosenstrasse. For a description of this heroic action, see p. 118.

The Empty Library

Bebelplatz (Unter den Linden between the Alte Bibliothek and the Deutsche Staatsoper. **Transportation:** *U-Bahn line U6 to Französische Strasse; Bus 100, 157, or 348 to Deutsche Staatsoper.*

This unusual memorial is dedicated to the notorious bookburning that took place on this site on May 10, 1933. In the middle of Bebelplatz, a small window is set flush into the paving stones. Beneath the glass is an empty, white room. The white room is lined with white shelves: an empty library, sterile and ghostly, a symbol of the books burned and the culture and knowledge lost. Plaques on either side of the glass explain: "On May, 10, 1933, in the middle of this plaza, National Socialist students burned the works of hundreds of free writers, journalists, philosophers and scientists." To the left is a quote from the poet Heinrich Heine: "Where one burns books, it is only a prelude; in the end one also burns people." "The "Empty Library" is by Israeli sculptor Micha Ullman.

An earlier plaque put up by the East German government and placed on the facade of the building on the western side of the square still stands, delivering a more doctrinaire account: "On this plaza Nazi brutishness destroyed the best works of German and world literature. The fascist bookburning of May 10, 1933 should be an eternal reminder to be vigilant against imperialism and war."

Herbert-Baum Gedenkstein
(Herbert Baum Memorial)

Lustgarten (Unter den Linden between the Zeughaus and the Berlin Cathedral). **Transportation:** *S-Bahn line S3, S5, S7, S9, or S75 to Hackescher Markt; Bus 100, 157, or 348 to Lustgarten.*

A memorial in the southeast corner of the Lustgarten plaza commemorates the Herbert Baum Group. The large stone cube recalls the best-known exploit of this Jewish communist resistance group, an arson attack on a Nazi propaganda exhibition that took place by this spot on May 18, 1942. The inscription reads: "Unforgotten, the courageous deeds and steadfastness of the antifascist resistance group led by the young communist Herbert Baum. Forever allied in friendship with the Soviet Union." The inscription makes it clear that the marker stems from the old communist government of East Germany, but while it lauds the communist nature of the Herbert Baum resistance group, it fails to take note of its Jewish character. The memorial was designed by Jürgen Raue and erected in 1981.

Max Reinhardt and Otto Brahm memorials

Schumannstrasse, in front of the Deutsches Theater. **Transportation:** *U-Bahn line U6 or S-Bahn line S3, S5, S7, S9, or S75 to Friedrichstrasse; Bus 147 to Schumannstrasse/Charité.*

These memorials commemorate Max Reinhardt and Otto Brahm, two pillars of modern German theater.

From 1894 to 1905, Brahm was director of the Deutsches Theater and helped to make Berlin one of Europe's theatrical centers. The director, who was also an influential critic and literary historian, was an exponent of the new naturalism and was a champion of Ibsen. The bust, from 1960, is by Eberhard Bachmann.

Stage producer and director Reinhardt was a giant of the theater in the first part of the twentieth century, and his experimental and often spectacular productions had an international influence. He was director of the Deutsche Theater from 1905 to 1932. In 1933, he immigrated to the United States, where he staged a notable production of *A Midsummer Night's Dream* in the Hollywood Bowl before 15,000 spectators, and later directed the popular film version with James Cagney and Mickey Rooney (1935). The sculpture is by Wilfried Fitzenreiter, from 1960.

Heinrich Heine Memorial

Volkspark am Weinberg, Veteranenstrasse. **Transportation:** *U-Bahn line U8 to Rosenthaler Platz; Tram 6, 8 or 50 to Brunnenstrasse/Invalidenstrasse.*

Whether or not Heinrich Heine, one of Germany's greatest poets, can or should be claimed as a Jew is a point that has been much debated. He converted to Protestantism in 1825 for practical, not religious, reasons—he called baptism "the entry ticket to Western civilization." Nevertheless, he was born a Jew and Judaism informs much of his writing. In 1850 he said: "I make no secret of my Judaism, to which I have not returned, because I never left it." One is, in any case, inclined to be liberal in the matter since this is one of the few monuments that celebrate a Jewish contribution to German culture, rather than mourning the destruction of the Jews.

Heine's political radicalism made him a favorite of the East Germans. This bronze sculpture, designed by Waldemar Grzimek and dedicated in 1966, shows the poet sitting. On the statue's base are friezes and the inscription: " 'We don't grasp ideas, ideas grasp us and enslave us and whip us into the arena so that we are forced to fight for them like gladiators.' Heinrich Heine, born Dec 13, 1797 in Düsseldorf, died Feb. 17, 1856 in Paris."

Memorial for the Martyrs of 1510

Mollstrasse 11. **Transportation:** *U-Bahn lines U2, U5, or U8, or S-Bahn lines S3, S5, S7, S9, or S75 to Alexanderplatz.*

There are some indications that a Jewish cemetery may have existed sometime between 1539 and 1571 in the vicinity of what is now Mollstrasse and Landwehrstrasse in the Prenzlauer Berg district of the city. No physical evidence exists on the site, but there are several eighteenth- and nineteenth-century (although no contemporary) reports of such a cemetery. There is a tradition, however, that the 38 innocent Jews burned to death in 1510 for supposedly desecrating a Host were buried here. Now standing in a small yard behind an apartment house at Mollstrasse 11 is a memorial plaque dating to 1935 (when it was erected in a nearby Jewish old-age home) honoring those victims. The Hebrew inscription reads: "Here lie the holy bones of the members of our first Jewish community in Berlin. They were murdered and burned as martyrs on the twelfth of Av, 5270." The German inscription beneath is a little more specific: "In the year 1510, 38 Berlin Jews were burned for alleged desecration of the Host. Their bones are buried here."

Garment District Memorial

Markgrafenstrasse 36. **Transportation:** *U-Bahn line U2 to Hausvogteiplatz; Bus 147 or 257 to Gendarmenmarkt.*

A modest memorial erected in late 1997 in the lobby of a building near Hausvogteiplatz, which at one time was the center of the garment district of Berlin. As in its counterpart in New York, Jewish firms and workers were found here in great numbers. "In remembrance of all Jews active in garment firms who were victims of National Socialist persecution," the inscription in a mirrored panel reads. Underneath is a list of some of those Jews who lost their lives in concentration camps. On the opposite wall, and reflected in the panel, are photographs of a garment firm building, workers inside a cutting room, even a clothing pattern. This memorial, by Christian Rothmann, is accessible only during business hours.

MOABIT

Levetzowstrasse Synagogue Memorial

Levetzowstrasse 7-8. **Transportation:** *U-Bahn line U9 to Hansaplatz; Bus 341 to Landesbildstelle.*

The Levetzowstrasse Synagogue was one of the largest and stateliest synagogues in Berlin, an imposing neo-classical structure seating 2,100. It was built in 1914 and featured a liberal service.

The synagogue was intended not only to serve congregants from the Moabit and Hansaviertel neighborhoods, but also to serve as major center for the Jewish community as a whole. The complex featured a religious school and living quarters. The Gestapo took advantage of the ample space and, since the synagogue suffered minimal damage during the Kristallnacht pogrom of November 9–10, 1938, turned it into a gathering point and detention center for deportations in 1941.

It was one of the major links in the chain of expulsion and destruction in Berlin. From here Jews were transported or marched to the Putlitzbrücke train station and forced into cattle cars for the journey to Theresienstadt, the ghettos of Lodz and Riga, and Auschwitz.

The Levetzowstrasse synagogue was severely damaged during the war and torn down in 1955.

At the corner of Levetzowstrasse and Jagowstrasse is a wall with a commemorative plaque, put up in 1960, that reads: "At this site stood a synagogue. It was destroyed on the terrible night of November 9, 1938. During the years of National Socialism, many of our Jewish fellow-citizens were forced to set out from here on their last path. Their memory is not forgotten."

In contrast to this simple plaque is the memorial on the other side of the plot, about 50 feet away on Levetzowstrasse. This is a massive, hulking sculpture of rusted steel and granite made of several large and distinct parts. In front is a representation, more or less life-size, of a railroad box car. Inside the rusty steel car, rough-hewn blocks of granite carved with human features are placed to represent huddled deportees. Behind this is a steel ramp, on top of which are four huge blocks of granite, again roughly representing human figures, buckled together with thick steel cable. Behind the ramp, 36 metal tiles are set into the ground. Most contain the names, addresses, and seating capacity of some of Berlin's pre-war synagogues as well as the dates of their dedica-tion and destruction.

Two of these tiles contain general information: "On this plot stood one of Berlin's largest synagogues. In 1941 the Jewish Community of Berlin was forced by the Gestapo to turn the building into a collection center. From here more than 37,500 Berlin Jews were deported from Grunewald and Putlitzstrasse train stations to the listed death camps. Furthermore, 14,797 Jews from the second-largest Berlin collection center, the former Jewish Old Age Home in Grosse Hamburger Strasse, were deported from Anhalter train station to Theresienstadt concentration camp in 117 transports from June 6, 1942 until March 27, 1945. In the pogrom night on November 9, 1938, the Jewish houses of worship were damaged, burned, destroyed. As symbols of an abundant Jewish cultural tradition in Prussia, they were the most important targets of the initial state-organized terror. In addition to the pictured Community and private synagogues there were over 80 private Jewish prayer houses or prayer halls in social institutions. These were also targets of devastation on the night of November 9, 1938 or a short time later closed, sold or expropriated."

Behind the carpet of tiles a huge stele looms like an Easter Island statue. Stenciled into the rusted iron plate is a list of 63 transports that departed from the synagogue while it was used by the Gestapo as a collection point for deportations. The destination of most of these transports was Auschwitz.

The whole thing is, at any rate, hard to miss. The memorial was constructed in 1988. It required three designers: Peter Herbrich, a sculptor, and two architects, Jürgen Wenzel and Theseus Bappert.

Deportation Mahnmal Putlitzbrücke
(Memorial to the Deportations at Putlitz Bridge)

Putlitzbrücke. **Transportation:** *U-Bahn line U9 to Birkenstrasse; Bus 127 to Birkenstrasse.*

This memorial commemorates the deportations that took place at the Putlitzbrücke railroad station, the largest of the Berlin deportation points, which was located below this bridge. Jews detained at the Levetzowstrasse synagogue were marched or trucked here and forced onto cattle cars for deportation and death in the camps in the east.

In 1987 the Berlin City Council sponsored the creation of this sculpture by Volkmar Haase. It consists of two asymetrical steles of brushed steel, one of which juts out over the train tracks below and is topped by a tangled staircase that end in mid-air. The other slab angles in the opposite direction, toward the bridge, and features a Star of David with an inscription. The text, fashioned to look like strips of telegram tape, reads: "Steps that are no longer steps, a staircase that is no longer a staircase; broken symbols of the roads that were no more. For those who were forced on their last path over ramps, train tracks, steps and staircases. Tens of thousands of Jewish fellow-citizens of Berlin were deported to and murdered in the death camps from Putlitzstrasse train station in the years 1941–44."

A small plaque to the left adds a depressing footnote:

"The memorial over the train tracks of the former Putlitzstrasse deportation train station was dedicated in 1987. Since then the target of defamatory desecrations, a bomb attack on August 29, 1992, heavily damaged parts of the memorial. Restored and rebuilt in March, 1993. Guilt that cannot be pardoned fills us with dismay. Never again."

NEUKÖLLN

Mahnmal für das KZ-Aussenlager Sonnenallee
(Memorialfor Sonnenallee Satellite Concentration Camp)

Sonnenallee 181-189. **Transportation:** *Bus 141 or 241 to Hertzbergplatz.*

This unusual memorial, installed by Norbert Rademacher in 1994, consists of a laser light that temporarily projects an "inscription" on the sidewalk when someone walks by at night.

Between 1942 and 1944, there was by this site a forced labor camp for the manufacture of munitions. After 1944, the camp was cleared to make way for 500 Jewish women, originally from the Lódz ghetto, transported from Ravensbrück concentration camp. This was one of more than 600 forced labor camps and 27 satellite concentration camps in Berlin. In April 1945, with the Russians approaching the city, the SS moved the women back to Ravensbrück. Most of this group was eventually rescued in Aktion Bernadotte, a rescue operation supervised by the Swedish Red Cross.

The inscription projected onto the sidewalk reads: "On this ground in 1942 the National Krupp Cash Register Corporation established a forced labor camp to supply armaments to the National Socialists. More than a hundred women were locked up here. From 1944–45 there were over 500 Jewish women from Poland in this camp. In these years there was a satellite camp of the Sachsenhausen concentration camp here."

SCHÖNEBERG

Orte des Erinnerns
(Places of Memories)

*Located throughout the "Bayerisches Viertel." **Transportation:** U-Bahn line U4 or U7 to Bayischerer Platz.*

This is one of Berlin's most unusual and effective memorials, though it does not recall a specific incident, mark a specific place, nor occupy a particular site. It is, rather, spread throughout the neighborhood, turning the entire area into a site of remembrance and reflection.

The memorial consists of eighty small signs posted on lamp posts throughout this neighborhood, which before the ascent of the Nazi government contained a large Jewish population. On one side of each sign is the text of an anti-Semitic Nazi law, an example of legal persecution, or, sometimes, excerpts from letters written by deported Jews. On the other side is a simple graphic icon that illustrates the text.

A sign with musical notation, for example, reads "Jews are expelled from singing clubs. August 16, 1933"; one depicting a clock reads "Jews may not leave their apartments after 8:00 in the evening (in summer 9:00). September 1, 1939"; another with a drawing of a loaf of bread (posted outside a market) reads "Jews are allowed to buy foodstuffs only from 4:00–5:00 in the afternoon. July 4, 1940."

The signs can be found on the several blocks encircling Bayerischer Platz. Large signboards with maps indicating the location of each sign can be found in Bayerischer Platz, in front of the Schöneberg City Hall, and in Münchener Strasse in front of the Scharmützelsee School. Folding maps can be picked up in the Schöneberg City Hall. The memorial, installed in 1993, is by Renata Stih and Frieder Schnock.

Münchner Strasse Synagogue Memorial

Münchener Strasse 37. **Transportation:** *U-Bahn line U4 or U7 to Bayerischer Platz.*

This sculpture, an understated arrangement of pale stone blocks by Gerson Fehrenbach, commemorates a small synagogue built by an independent Orthodox group, the "Schoeneberg Synagogue Association". The sculpture, erected in 1963, was the first official memorial in Berlin to commemorate an aspect of the city's destroyed Jewish community. The inscription reads: "Here stood the synagogue of the Jewish community built in 1909." At the base of the sculpture another plaque, added later, explains: "From 1909–56 a synagogue stood here. Because of its location in an apartment house, it was not destroyed during the night of the pogrom on November 9, 1938. After the National Socialist expulsion and destruction of Jewish fellow citizens, it lost its function and was torn down in 1956."

Concentration Camps Memorial plaques

Wittenbergplatz. **Transportation:** *U-Bahn line U1, U2, or U15 to Wittenbergplatz, Bus 119, 129, 146, or 219 to Wittenbergplatz.*

Kaiser-Wilhelm-Platz. **Transportation:** *U-Bahn line U7 to Kleistpark; Bus 104, 148, 187, or 348 to Kaiser-Wilhelm-Platz.*

These simple but powerful signs, identical and set in busy shopping areas, are reminders of 12 concentration and extermination camps. The inscription reads: "Places of terror that we must never forget: Auschwitz, Stutthof, Maidanek, Treblinka, Theresienstadt, Buchenwald, Dachau, Sachsenhausen, Ravensbrück, Bergen-Belsen, Trostenez, Flossenbürg."

It is interesting that in a country that spends so much time searching for unusual and "appropriate" aesthetic forms for its Holocaust memorials, these workmanlike signs should be among its most visible and direct. No symbols, no metaphors—just a simple declaration. The signs were erected in 1967 on the initiative of

A. Only

This modest memorial to the destroyed Münchener Strasse Synagogue was one of the first in the city.

the League for Human Rights, partially in response to one of the first postwar memorials, a large signboard that commemorated the lost "German" cities of Königsberg, Danzig, and others. (That sign stood from 1952 to 1972.)

STEGLITZ

Spiegelwand
(Mirror Wall)

Hermann-Ehlers-Platz. ***Transportation:*** *U-Bahn line U9 or S-Bahn line 1 to Rathaus Steglitz; Bus 148, 170, 180, 185, 186, 188, 280, 285, or 383 to Rathaus Steglitz.*

This memorial to the Jewish residents of the Steglitz district consists of a large wall, 11 1/2 feet high by 36 feet wide, of steel polished to a mirror finish. The wall is covered by a great deal of text, most of it a listing of deported Jews, and a number of pictures with captions.

The monument, designed by Wolfgang Göschel, Joachim von Rosenberg, and Hans-Norbert Burkert was put up in June 1995. During the planning stage, it aroused fierce resistance from local officials and neighborhood activists. Although arguments were, for the most part, couched in aesthetic terms, it was clear that much of the opposition found the monument an obtrusive reminder of a past they would rather ignore or forget. After the local district council rejected the monument, the embarrassed city government stepped in to complete the project.

The very long historical introduction at the top left corner of the front (north) side reads:

> The Jews in Germany are a small minority of less than one percent of the total population. In 1933, 3,186 members of the Jewish religious community live in Berlin-Steglitz. In National Socialist-ruled Germany, people were characterized as inferior according to the measure of an alleged "blood purity." Citizens long having equal rights became the object of a "racial separation" of Jews and Germans. Expulsions from jobs, disenfranchisement, finally prohibitions against emigration and forced labor are the prelude to arbitrary arrest, deportation and murder during the years from 1941 to 1945. From October 18, 1941 until March 27, 1945, 61 so-called eastern-transports and 121 so-called elder-transports are sent from Berlin to the ghettos and extermination camps of Auschwitz, Kovno, Lodz, Minsk, Reval, Riga, Theresienstadt, Warsaw and the district of Lublin.
>
> In the following, the names, dates of birth and addresses of

1,723 Berliners, persecuted because of their race, are documented as they are listed on the preserved transport lists. The additional middle names Israel and Sara, which were forced upon Jews by the Nazis in 1939, have been deliberately removed. Along with each transport, the date of deportation from Berlin and, as far as it is known, the destination, is given. Those persecuted because of their race, who earlier had to leave Steglitz, Lankwitz, Lichterfelde and Südende because of compulsory transfer into so-called Jewish dwellings, are not recognizable on those lists as inhabitants of Steglitz.

Those pages of the Berlin transport lists, so far as they contain addresses from Steglitz, are offered. Unreadable names had to be left off. It becomes clear that the deportation of 230 citizens from Steglitz is only a selection of the deportation and murder of nearly 50,000 Berlin Jews.

Some of the racially persecuted survived in so-called mixed marriages, a few returned from the ghettos and extermination camps, even fewer could survive underground.

On the left side is a photo of a former local synagogue and a chronology of the synagogue, local Jewish history, and the evolution of the "Speigelwand" memorial itself. The synagogue, still extant, is located in the backyard of Düppelstrasse 41, directly to your left. It is now in use as an office, but the exterior has been restored to its original appearance. Access is possible only during weekdays.

In the middle of the wall is a photo of two children lighting a menorah. The caption explains: "Children with Chanukah candles. Ruth and Georg Pisarek light the lamp on Chanukah. Photo from the photo archive of the photographer Abraham Pisarek (1901–83), the father of the children. They survived in Berlin."

On the right side is a quotation from Robert M. W. Kempner, a Berliner who later fled to the United States and returned to Germany as chief U.S. prosecutor in the Nuremberg Trials. It reads: "Men took away their occupations, stole their property, they were not allowed to inherit or bequeath, they were not allowed to sit on park benches or to keep a canary, could not use public transportation, could visit no restaurants, no concerts, theaters or movie houses, specific racial laws were applied to them, they were deprived of all their civil rights, their freedom of movement was taken away from them, their human rights and human dignity were ground to

The Spiegelwand (Mirror Wall) in Steglitz, its reflective surface meant to spark reflection.

dust, until they were deported to concentration camps and sent to the gas chambers...The victims were Jews. The yellow star marked them."

On the other (south) side, there are more pictures among the deportation lists. On the left side is a photo of the New Synagogue before its restoration. The caption reads: "The New Synagogue on Oranienburger Strasse in the center of Berlin was designed and built by the architects Eduard Knoblauch and August Stüler. On September 5, 1866, following seven years of construction, there is a ceremonial opening. The synagogue is the architectural expression of the self-assurance of the Berlin Jews. On the night of November 9–10, 1938, the inspector of the police headquarters in charge, Wilhelm Krützfeld, prevented the SA from setting it on fire to a greater extent. The building was heavily damaged in bombing raids in the Second World War. The picture shows the ruins in 1988. Photo: Günther Krawutschke."

On the far right side is another photo of the New Synagogue, this one after its restoration. This caption reads: "New Synagogue reconstruction. In 1988 the "New Synagogue-Centrum Judaica" Foundation was established. In the same year, rebuilding and reconstruction begins. The architect is Bernhard Leisering. The rebuilding testifies to the tolerance of the majority, in the midst of which the Jewish community can lead their own religious life—at the same time being integrated in the life and culture of the surrounding society. With the reconstruction of the cupola the architects returned to Berlin part of its silhouette. Photo: Stefan Erhard. 1994."

In the middle of this side is a panel that asks: "and today?" Although the wall's polished surface, in which viewers can see themselves, is immediately striking, the many disparate and seemingly random elements thrown together to compose the memorial—as well as the odd phrasing of the texts—results in the lack of a cohesive point.

TIERGARTEN

Memorial for the Adass Yisroel Congregation at Siegmundshof

Wullenwebersteg footbridge. **Transportation:** *S-Bahn line S3, S5, S7, S9, or S75 to Tiergarten.*

This memorial commemorates the former Adass Yisroel synagogue and primary and secondary schools that once stood nearby at Siegmundshof 11.

The German inscription on the monument, a stylized menorah by George Seibert dedicated in 1986, reads: "Israelite Synagogue-Congregation 'Adass Yisroel' of Berlin. Co-founded by Rabbi Dr. Esriel Hildesheimer as an enlightened Orthodox congregation in 1869. Here on the Jewish New Year 5685 (1924) a school building and synagogue were dedicated. In 1939 all the congregation facilities were broken up. Members, teachers and students were stripped of their rights and tormented, many taken away and killed. Blessed is the remembrance of the just. Berlin, June 25, 1986."

The other side of the monument notes the names and addresses of the several synagogues, schools and institutions of the Adass Yisroel congregation.

A plaque nearby delivers a history of the congregation in Hebrew, German, and English. It was installed on the New Year 5759 (1998), 75 years after the dedication of the original building.

Memorial to Rosa Luxemburg

South side of the Landwehrkanal under the Lichtensteinbrücke (in the Tiergarten park). **Transportation:** *U-Bahn line U2 or U9, or S-Bahn line S3, S5, S7, S9, S75 to Zoologischer Garten; Bus 100, 109, 145, 146, 149, 245,* *or 249 to Zoologischer Garten.*

This monument for the revolutionary leader Rosa Luxemburg is placed at the spot where her body was thrown into the canal by right-wing paramilitary troops in January 1919. Rosa Luxemburg, a Polish-born Jew, was a theoretician especially noted for her critique of imperialism. She was a leader of the Spartacus Workers' movement, which sought to establish a Soviet republic in Germany, and remains a hero not only to communists but also to many left-wing Social Democrats and feminists. The sculpture, by Ralf Schüler and Ursulina Schüler-Witte, was built in 1987.

WILMERSDORF

Grunewald Deportations Memorial

Am Bahnhof Grunewald. **Transportation:** *S-Bahn line S3 or S7 to Grunewald; Bus 186 to Grunewald.*

The Grunewald train station was one of three deportation points in Berlin (Putlitzstrasse and Anhalter train stations were the other two) for some 55,000 Jewish victims of the Nazis. Beginning in October 1941, Jews were marched openly through the streets to these stations, initially to be transported to the ghettos of Lodz, Riga, Warsaw, and elsewhere in the east, where most were killed by SS units or taken to death camps. After mid-1942, they were sent directly to Auschwitz.

A large concrete block set into the hillside with human figures scooped out of its face and disappearing into its depth, was created by Karol Broniatowski and installed in 1991. Next to it, an inscription on a stele reads: "In remembrance of the more than 50,000 Berlin Jews who, between October 1941 and February 1945, were deported, primarily from Grunewald freight depot, by the National Socialist state and murdered in its death camps. To admonish us, to oppose courageously and without hesitation every disregard of life and human dignity."

Gleis 17
(Track 17)

Am Bahnhof Grunewald. **Transportation:** *S-Bahn line S3 or S7 to Grunewald; Bus 186 to Grunewald.*

Another, more recent, monument can also be found at the Grunewald train station by continuing up the slope past the above sculpture and turning left. This simple and effective memorial, called "Track 17," consists of a long series of large iron plates laid out on the ground on both sides of a train spur. As you walk on the plates alongside and just above the track, you can read, written on the side of each plate, the date, destination, and number of Jews deported for each transport that left here between 1941 and 1945. The old track that carried the trains, now overgrown with trees and shrubs, is integrated into the monument as both historical artifact and artistic metaphor. The piece was designed by the architectural team of Hirsch, Lorch and Wandel.

At the other end of the walkway of iron panels is another plaque. This was put up in 1987, several years before the "Track 17" memorial was installed, by the Berlin city council. The German inscription reads "To the memory of the tens of thousands of Berlin Jewish citizens who, from October 1941 to February 1945, were deported to and murdered in the death camps by the Nazi executioners." The Hebrew inscription on top reads simply: "To the memory of the victims of the Shoah."

Walther Rathenau Memorial

Koenigsallee at the corner of Erdener Strasse. **Transportation:** *Bus 119 to Erdener Strasse.*

Walther Rathenau was head of the huge AEG electrical company (the General Electric of Germany) and later one of the most prominent public servants of the Weimar Republic. He was appointed Foreign Minister in February 1922—the highest political office ever achieved by a Jew in Germany. Rathenau was assassinated four months later at this spot by right-wing nationalists who, under the Nazis, were lauded as national heroes.

A simple granite marker set in a small cobbled space marks the spot. The plaque, one of the first post-war memorials, reads: "The Liberal Democratic Party of Germany/To the memory of Walther Rathenau/Foreign Minister of the German [Weimar] Republic/He fell on this spot at the hands of murderers on June 24, 1922. 'The health of a people comes only from its inner life—from the life of its soul and its spirit.' October 1946." Rathenau lived about a mile down the road at Koenigsallee 65; a small plaque on the front railing identifies the house.

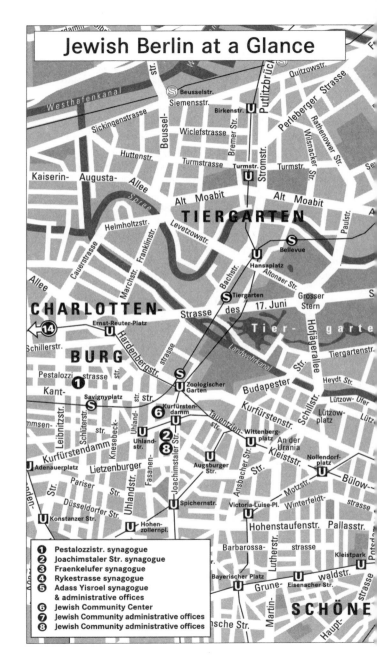

Jewish Berlin at a Glance

❶ Pestalozzistr. synagogue
❷ Joachimstaler Str. synagogue
❸ Fraenkelufer synagogue
❹ Rykestrasse synagogue
❺ Adass Yisroel synagogue
   & administrative offices
❻ Jewish Community Center
❼ Jewish Community administrative offices
❽ Jewish Community administrative offices

⑨	New Synagogue – Centrum Judaicum Foundation
⑩	Jewish Communication Center
⑪	Grosse Hamburger Str. cemetery
⑫	Schönhauser Allee cemetery
⑬	Weissensee cemetery & Adass Yisroel cemetery (offmap)
⑭	Heerstrasse cemetery (offmap)
⑮	Jewish Museum (open 2000)

"GESTAPO, SS, AND REICH SECURITY MAIN OFFICE ON THE *PRINZ ALBRECHT GROUNDS*" – A DOCUMENTATION

Between 1933 and 1945, the central offices of the Nazi regime's most important surveillance and persecuting systems were located on the "Prinz Albrecht Grounds" between Stresemannstraße, Niederkirchnerstraße (formerly Prinz-Albrecht-Straße), Wilhelmstraße, and Anhalter Straße:

- the Secret State Police Office (Gestapo)
- the SS leadership
- the SA leadership for Berlin/Brandenburg (1934–1939)
- the Security Service (SD) of the SS
- the Reich Security Main Office (from 1939 on).

After the war, the grounds were levelled and later put to commercial use. Not until 1987 was it made accessible to the public as the "Topography of Terror". Excavations and information plaques provide information on the material traces and historical character of the grounds. The exhibition opened in 1987 documents the history of the site, the Nazi institutions located here, and the crimes committed, ordered, or planned here.

TOPOGRAPHY OF TERROR

Stresemannstraße 110 · 10963 Berlin
daily 10 a.m. to 6 p.m., may until september 10 a.m. to 8 p.m.
admission free · public transportation connections:
Bus 341, 129, 248 · S-Bahn Anhalter Bahnhof
U- and S-Bahn Potsdamer Platz · U-Bahn Kochstraße
tours by appointment · telephone 254 86-703 · fax 262 71 56

Due to construction work, the exhibition can be viewed as an open-air presentation until the new visitor and information center is opened.

9 | Third Reich Sites

Several notorious places associated with the Nazi regime remain extant. Some have now become memorials or museums and play a penitential role of sorts. Others, such as Goering's *Luftwaffe* (air force) headquarters and the Olympic Stadium, are still in use.

The country is ambivalent about many of these "landmarks." It recognizes that some sort of remembrance is necessary, yet is often reluctant to set these places aside as memorials. There is sometimes a feeling that too much attention is paid to the Nazi past and that too many resources are devoted to the restoration or maintenance of Third Reich structures.

There is the fear too that Nazi sites will either become places of veneration by rightists or targets of attack by leftists. Thus Spandau Prison, where Hitler's deputy Rudolph Hess was so long imprisoned, was torn down immediately after his death. And similar fears animated a controversy that broke out in 1995 over whether to preserve recently found murals in a surviving portion of Hitler's bunker. (For the time being they have been saved but are inaccessible.)

Of course these sites are not strictly a part of "Jewish Berlin," yet their impact on the city's Jews was so decisive, and the face of Berlin—indeed of all of Europe—so altered by their presence that it would be inappropriate to exclude them.

■ Hitler's Bunker

The site of the bunker where Hitler spent his last desperate moments as his thousand-year Reich disintegrated, and where he committed suicide on April 30, 1945, is unmarked and unnoted. The bunker was blown up and leveled by the Soviets after the war. Because the site was later subsumed within the no-man's land just behind the Berlin Wall, it has remained basically undeveloped.

The bunker once stood, more or less, on an area now covered by a parking lot and grassy plot behind Wilhelmstrasse 90-92.

Topographie des Terrors
(Topography of Terror)
Stresemannstrasse 110 (tel: 254 86703). **Transportation:** *S-Bahn line S1, S2, or S25 to Anhalter Bahnhof; Bus 129, 248, or 341 to Anhalter Bahnhof;* **Open:** *Daily 10am–6pm.*
This museum, located over the unearthed basement of an annex to

Gestapo headquarters, is devoted to the history of state terror during the Third Reich.

With original documents and contemporary photographs, it charts the origins, structure, development, and gruesome deeds of the Gestapo (the secret state police); the SS (*Schutzstaffel*, literally the defense staff, but actually the Nazi party army); the SA (*Sturmabteilung*, literally storm troopers, the party militia) the SD (*Sicherheitsdienst*, the security service, another internal security office) and the Reich Security Main Office, which coordinated these sometimes competing groups. All of these organizations had offices in the area immediately surrounding the museum. It was here that preparations for the Wannsee Conference were made and here where the *Einsatzgruppen*, the special units that carried out mass murders in eastern Europe, were formed.

Gunther Schneider

The basement of the *Gestapo* headquarters were used as a place of detention and torture. The site is now the Topography of Terror museum.

Gestapo headquarters were located at Prince-Albrecht-Strasse 8, just north of the present museum, in a building destroyed during the war. In the late 1970s, the site, long a rubble-strewn lot, was "rediscovered" and, after several years of public debate, it was finally decided in 1987 to erect a temporary pavilion containing an exhibition detailing the history of the site.

It is only now, more than ten years after the construction of the pavilion, that a permanent home is being prepared for the Topography of Terror. While this is being built, the exhibition is temporarily located outside. The new building should be ready to open at the end of 2000.

The exhibition consists mainly of enlarged documents, photographs, and organizational charts. Though the presentation is often dry, the slow accumulation of detail becomes increasingly distressing. The exhibit is in German; however, an English-language catalog, with the texts translated, is available.

The exhibition continues outside where, in a roofed-over excavation next to the pavilion, the foundations of cells of the former Gestapo prison can be seen. In the adjoining field a series of plaques, with texts in German and English, point out the location of the Nazi-regime buildings that were clustered in this neighborhood. The Topography of Terror is erecting a new building here to replace its present modest pavilion, but the plaques should remain undisturbed.

Incidentally, the north side of the field is the location of one of the largest extant stretches of the Berlin Wall.

Gedenkstätte und Museum Sachsenhausen
(Sachenhausen Memorial and Museum)

Strasse der Nationen 22, Oranienburg (tel: 033 010 3715). **Transportation:** *S-Bahn line S1 to Oranienburg. Then walk east on Strasse des Friedens, turn left into Strasse der Einheit to Strasse der Nationen.* **Open:** *April 1–September 30: daily 8:30am–6pm; October 1–March 31: daily 8:30am–4:30pm. Exhibitions are closed on Mondays.* Located just about 12 miles (20km) outside of Berlin, Sachsenhausen was one of the first concentration camps built by the Nazis, and also one of the longest-lived, having been put to use after the war by the Soviets. Although it is not classified as an "extermination camp," there was an facility here—known as Station Z—where prisoners were executed. Of the approximately 204,000 inmates imprisoned in this camp during the years of the Third Reich, almost 100,000 were systematically put to death.

Sachsenhausen concentration camp was opened in 1936. The earliest prisoners were communists, social democrats, trade unionists, and other political opponents of the Nazi government, as well as pacifists and Jehovah's Witnesses. The first German Jews were imprisoned here in 1938. Later that year some 6,000 Jews from Berlin, Hamburg, and other locales were rounded up in the wake of the Kristallnacht pogrom and interned here. From 1938–40 the commandant of the camp was Rudolf Höss, later in charge of Auschwitz.

With the outbreak of World War II, thousands of "stateless" and Polish Jews, as well as political prisoners, were imprisoned here. Over the course of the war, prisoners from all over Europe were shipped to Sachsenhausen, eventually turning it into the second most populous German concentration camp. A head count on January 30, 1945 recorded 58,147 prisoners.

Sachsenhausen supplied slave labor for the armaments industry, and many inmates were sent out of the main camp to work in satellite camps or factories, some of them in Berlin. Prisoners were also used as guinea pigs for pseudo-medical experiments.

The camp was the site of an inspiring, if ultimately futile, uprising by Jewish prisoners on October 22, 1942. On that day, the 450 Jews then remaining in the camp, rather than being summoned to assemble for work, were instead taken to the disinfection hut. Believing that they were about to be liquidated, a small group of eighteen, most of them members of the communist-led resistance group operating in the camp, decided to go out fighting.

They smashed through a window and ran towards the roll call area, yelling and knocking down the guards who rushed to subdue them. Contrary to their expectations, the SS officer in charge ordered that no shots be fired, and for several minutes the prisoners grappled fiercely with the guards before they were overpowered. They assumed they were to be shot immediately, but the camp commandant inexplicably merely marched them back to the roll call grounds.

That month they, along with almost all other Jewish prisoners in the camp, were transferred to Auschwitz. Only those Jews involved in a secret and curious project remained: a Nazi counterfeiting operation producing forgeries of British, American, and Yugoslav banknotes as well as business papers and postage stamps for use by the Gestapo. Beginning in the summer of 1944, however, Jewish prisoners again began to arrive in the camp.

On April 21, 1945, the SS evacuated the camp, marching 33,000 prisoners north toward the Baltic Sea. They planned to pack them aboard ships which they would then sink. Though the SS never reached the sea, this forced march claimed the lives of some 6,000 prisoners. The camp was liberated by the Soviet Army on April 22, 1945.

By the end of the summer the Soviets began to use the camp, at first for Nazi prisoners, but more and more for political opponents. All told, some 50,000 to 60,000 prisoners passed through the Soviet "Special Camp Number 7" until its closure in March, 1950. Recently a mass grave of some of the 20,000 prisoners who died in Special Camp Number 7 was uncovered in the forest nearby.

The East German government reopened Sachsenhausen in 1961 as a memorial site. A towering stone obelisk entitled "Liberation," by René Graetz, was erected in the middle of the camp and a museum built just outside the present entrance to the grounds. Special and temporary exhibitions (occasionally but not often with English translations) are housed in the museum, which also contains a memorial wall.

A few original fragments from the camp have survived. Among these are the tower above the (partially reconstructed) main gate, which bears the slogan found in almost all concentration camps: *Arbeit Macht Frei* (work makes you free).

Beyond the gate on the far right is a wing of the cell block, partially reconstructed, that housed a Gestapo special prison. The small cells, often completely darkened, were used for punishment or to house important internees. Here the camp's most prominent prisoner, the opposition clergyman Martin Niemöller, was held. Niemöller is the author of the famous lines: "When the Nazis came for the Communists I was silent, for I wasn't a Communist. When the Nazis came for the Social Democrats I was silent, for I wasn't a Social Democrat. When the Nazis came for the Trade Unionists I was silent, for I wasn't a Trade Unionist. When the Nazis came for the Jews I was silent, for I wasn't a Jew. When the Nazis came for me there was no one left to protest." Several of the cells now contain memorial plaques, donated by various countries, to those once incarcerated here.

The former inmates' kitchen houses a museum, dating from the communist era, that traces the history of the camp. It evinces the musty militance typical of such communist displays, and the German text is not translated. The foundations of "Station Z," which included a gas chamber and crematorium, have also been preserved. The building itself, and appurtenances, were demolished in 1953. The "Pathologie" survives too, where doctors carried out pseudo-medical experiments on inmates. There is a small exhibit here (with English translations) of gruesome photographs.

Two barracks used exclusively for Jewish prisoners, Barracks 38 & 39, were reconstructed in 1961 and once housed a special exhibit on Jewish inmates. In September 1992, shortly after a visit to the camp by Israeli Prime Minister Itzhak Rabin, arsonists set fire to these barracks, almost completely destroying them. Two years later, two young neo-Nazi skinheads were sentenced to short prison terms for the deed.

In late 1997, the barracks were reopened. They feature an exhibition that incorporates evidence of the arson attack, considered now to be part of the "history" of the barracks. This was thought to be a fitter solution than merely reconstructing the buildings yet again. The charred walls of Barrack 38 are preserved behind glass, through which one can see, in the blackened interior, the bunk beds and tables in their original positions. The exhibition itself, next door, consists in large part of personal items of prisoners—shoes and suitcases, for example—and snippets of recollections and testimonies. A special exhibit is dedicated to the counterfeiting workshop, which was manned mostly by Jews. The exhibition in Barrack 39 concentrates on presenting a sense of the daily routines and horrors of prisoners' lives.

Flyers in English are available. English-language guided tours can be arranged by calling the memorial center office.

Mahn- und Gedenkstätte Ravensbrück
(Ravensbrück Memorial Museum)

*Strasse der Nationen, Fürstenberg (tel: 0330 933 9241). **Transportation:** Train from Berlin-Lichtenberg train station to Stralsund. From there a walk (circa 2 miles/3km) or a taxi ride to the museum; **Open:** Tuesday–Sunday 9am–5pm; memorial grounds open until 6pm.*

Ravensbrück was set up by the Nazis as a camp exclusively for women, the only large-scale one of its kind on German soil. The first prisoners, criminals and Jehovah's Witnesses, arrived on May 15, 1939, soon after the camp was completed by inmates from Sachsenhausen. A shipment of political prisoners, some of whom were Jewish, arrived three days later. The number of Jews held here continued to rise until October, 1942, when all Jewish prisoners were sent to Auschwitz or Majdenek. However, less than two years later, in the summer of 1944, Hungarian Jewish women were incarcerated here, to be followed later by others tranferred from other camps.

A total of 132,000 women and children and 20,000 men—who were incarcerated in an annex to the camp built in April, 1941—passed through Ravensbrück. About 15% of the inmates were Jewish. Some 92,000 died here.

Some of these fatalities were the result of gruesome pseudo-medical experiments; other inmates fell victim to the Nazi "14f13" project, a "euthanasia" operation in which Jews, handicapped, and those considered unable to work were shipped in December 1941 to Auschwitz and murdered. In the fall of 1944, a gas chamber was constructed and over 5,000 prisoners were sent to their deaths there. Ravensbrück was not, however, considered an extermination camp.

In April, 1945, some 7,000 prisoners were released from Ravensbrück and sent to Switzerland and Sweden in a deal brokered by Swedish Count Bernadotte, the Red Cross and the World Jewish Congress. At least 1,000 of these women saved at the eleventh hour were Jewish.

With the approach of the Soviet army in the last weeks of April, tens of thousands of women were forced out of the camp on a death march headed north toward the Baltic Sea. Thousands died of starvation and exhaustion. On April 30, 1945, the Red Army liberated the camp.

The Ravensbrück National Memorial Museum opened on September 12, 1959, although much of the camp continued to be used as quarters by the Soviet army, which did not withdraw from its base here until February 1994.

The focal point of the memorial is the large bronze sculpture by Will Lammert, *Tragende* (The Burdened Woman). Overlooking the tranquil Schwedt Lake, it provides a rare vista for reflection. Behind it is a large rose garden, the site of a mass grave of prisoners, with several memorial stones; one is for the Jewish inmates murdered here. Behind the garden rises a large brick wall, an original artifact of the camp, now designated the "Wall of Nations," and including the names of the 20 countries from which prisoners originated.

The barracks, which comprised the largest part of the camp, no longer exist, but several of the original buildings are extant. The commandant's headquarters, the first building you'll see on your left as you enter the grounds, now houses the main exhibitions, "Ravensbrück: Topography and History of the Concentration Camp for Women," a general overview of the camp, and "Ravensbrück Women," biographies of 27 representative inmates. Both are in German only but contain many photos and artifacts.

Behind the commandant's headquarters is a block of prison cells used by the SS for special punishment. As in Sachsenhausen, the cells now house small memorials donated by the various countries from which prisoners came. Cells are also devoted to Sinti and Roma, Jews, and the victims of the July 20, 1944 plot against Hitler. Next to the cell block stands the crematorium, built in April 1943.

Going around the right side of the commandant's office takes you through the original gates of the camp. Just before the entrance, you'll find the camp's original waterworks and garages, now used for the display of temporary exhibits. The roll call area, witness to much misery and death, lies just beyond the gates.

Brochures in English are available, as are, by prior arrangement, English-language guided tours.

Gedenkstätte Plötzensee
(Plötzensee Memorial)

Hüttigpfad (tel: 344 3226). **Transportation:** *Bus 123 to Gedenkstätte Plötzensee;* **Open:** *March–September: daily 8am–6pm; Winter months: daily 8:30am until dusk.*

Plötzensee Prison, now given over to use as a "juvenile corrective establishment," was used by the Nazis for incarcerating and executing political, religious and "racial" opponents of the fascist government. Between 1933 and 1945, some 2,500 people were executed here. A memorial, which includes the original building used for executions, was established here by the Berlin city council in 1952. It was the first "official," i.e. non-private, memorial established in the city.

The first section of the memorial consists of an enclosed, flag-stoned courtyard with a large wall at one end. "To the victims of the Hitler Dictatorship of 1933–1945," the inscription reads. Buried beneath the foundation is a scroll upon which is written: "During the years of the Hitler dictatorship, from 1933 to 1945, hundreds of human beings were put to death by judicial murder on this spot. They died because they chose to fight against the dictatorship for human rights and political freedom. They included people from every walk of life and nearly every country. Through this memorial, Berlin honors those millions of victims of the Third Reich who, because of their political convictions, religious beliefs, or racial origins, were vilified, abused, deprived of their freedom, or murdered."

On the right side of the courtyard a large stone urn is set. The small plaque before it states: "This urn contains earth from German concentration camps."

Passing behind the wall on the right side will take you to the execution building. The execution room remains, and has been restored, more or less to its wartime condition. Five hooks hang from a wooden beam. Originally there were eight, as well as a guillotine, but otherwise the room is much as it was.

Well known as the site where many of those involved in the July 20, 1944 plot against Hitler were hanged, this is also where 22 members of the Herbert Baum resistance group were executed between August 18, 1942 and September 7, 1943.

A second room features a small exhibit with documents of the Nazi courts, including death warrants and other legal papers. An English-language brochure is available here. It does not, however, translate the exhibits in the room, but contains instead a brief account of anti-Nazi resistance, with an emphasis on the July 20, 1944 military plot.

Gedenkstätte Haus der Wannsee-Konferenz
(Wannsee Conference House Memorial)

*Am Großen Wannsee 56-58 (tel: 805 0010). **Transportation:** S-Bahn line S1 or S3 to Wannsee, then bus 114 to Haus der Wannsee-Konferenz; **Open:** Monday–Friday 10am–6pm, Saturday–Sunday 2pm–6pm.*

Landesbildstelle Berlin

The House Wannsee Conference House Memorial now hosts a study center and exhibition.

The Wannsee area has long been a popular lakeside resort where Berliners flock for sailing, swimming, and picnicking. Its name now, however, is also associated with the notorious "Wannsee Conference."

On January 20, 1942, Reinhard Heydrich, chief of the Gestapo and the SD (the security service of the SS), chaired a meeting of 14 top civil servants and SS officers in this villa to discuss and coordinate the "final solution" of the Jews of Europe.

In 1992, on the 50th anniversary of the conference, this memorial and educational center was opened. The permanent exhibition, which winds through almost a dozen rooms in the mansion, provides a solid if cursory chronological introduction to Nazi policies and practices toward the Jews: persecution; deportation; ghettoization; execution; the concentration and death camps; and the other grim stations of genocide. Contemporary photographs, newspapers, and Nazi party and German army papers document the appalling sweep of destruction and murder through Europe.

The largest room, originally the villa's dining room, is dominated by a large table and affords splendid views, past a sloping green yard, of the Wannsee lake. It was in this room that the conference was held, and around a similar table that Reinhard Heydrich, Roland Freisler, Heinrich Müller, Adolf Eichmann and other government officials calmly discussed the extermination of European Jewry. "In the course of the Final Solution," the surviving minutes of the meeting state, "the Jews are to be sent in a suitable manner and under appropriate supervision to labor in the east. Separated by sexes, Jews able to work will be led in large labor columns into these areas while building roads. In the process, large numbers will undoubtedly drop out through natural attrition." Some of the original leaves of these chilling notes are on display.

The text of the exhibition is in German but an English-language catalog that translates the commentary and many of the contemporary documents can be purchased or borrowed at the front desk. Guided tours in English are also available by appointment.

In addition to this permanent exhibition, the center also maintains an educational department that offers workshops and seminars, generally geared toward school classes, and a library with research material on National Socialism, Jewish history, and anti-Semitism, a great deal of it in English.

**Olympiastadion
(Olympic Stadium)**

*Olympischer Platz (tel: 300 633). **Transportation:** U-Bahn line U2 to Olympia-stadion (Ost); Bus 218 to Olympischer Platz; **Open:** Daily 9am–5pm.*
This huge stadium—it can seat up to 90,000 spectators—was built as a Nazi showcase for the 1936 Summer Olympics and is still in use for sporting events. Designed by Werner March, it is, with its massive pillars, soaring towers, and sleek stone facing, a quintessential example of Nazi monumental architecture. At the time of its construction, it was the largest stadium in the world.

The Nazi penchant for massed pageantry melded perfectly with the Olympic fondness for spectacle, and the German government took advantage of the opportunities afforded by the 1936 Olympics to demonstrate the vivacity, popularity and moderation of the National Socialist revolution.

The government's anti-Semitism was downplayed during the Olympics but it still proved to be a cause of concern. Even before the games there were calls, most significantly from the US, for a boycott. The American Olympic Committee approved participation in the Games by only a slim majority, and only after pressuring Germany to ensure that Jewish athletes would be allowed to participate.

Nazi assurances were meaningless, of course, though one "token Jew," Helene Mayer, a champion fencer, was allowed on the German team. (Another, ice hockey player Rudi Ball, played in that year's winter games in Garmisch-Partenkirchen.) Mayer (with a gentile mother, she was not halachically Jewish) took a silver medal. Despite the boycott campaign, many Jews did participate, taking a total of 8 medals (not including Mayer's silver) in what must have been extremely intimidating circumstances.

The stunning performance of the African-American Jesse Owens —four gold medals—is often cited as a humiliation for the Nazis and a blow to their theories of racial superiority. At the time however, the Games were perceived as a great success for Nazi Germany. The German teams took the largest number of medals of any country. The world saw a revitalized Germany and a very popular government, a virile state capable of managing the largest and most spectacular Olympic Games ever held. Still, today, fittingly, it is Jesse Owens who is remembered.

Haus der Wannsee-Konferenz

Gedenk- und Bildungsstätte

Am Grossen Wannsee 56-58 • D – 14109 Berlin
Telefon (030) 80 50 01 - 0 • Telefax (030) 80 50 01 27

The Historical Site
On January 20th, 1942 Reinhard Heydrich,
Head of the NS Reich Security Main Office
(Reichssicherheitshauptamt), chaired a meeting
of fourteen high-ranking civil servants and
SS-officers in this villa.
As the decision to murder the Europeans Jews
had been made earlier, the »Wannsee
Conference« was concerned with the
organization and implementation of »The Final
Solution«, the decision to deport the Jews of
Europe to the East and to murder them. The
meeting has become known as the »Wannsee
Conference«, taking its name from this district
of Berlin.

Exhibition
The Wannsee Conference and the Genocide of
the European Jews

Hours:
Monday to Friday   10.00 am – 6.00 pm
Saturday, Sunday   2.00 pm – 6.00 pm
Admission free. Guided tours by appointment only.

Media Center
Reference library, videotape collection, audiovisual archives
Monday to Friday 10.00 am – 6.00 pm

Workshops and seminars by appointment only.

Public transportation:
S-Bahn station »Wannsee«, then bus 114 to House of the
Wannsee Conference

---

10 | Genealogy & Property Claims

Carrying out genealogical research in Berlin can be an arduous task. Researchers should come well-prepared and allow plenty of time. Records are incomplete and sources and archives are scattered among various district and administrative units and in other cities and countries.

A case in point is the information that you are most likely to be searching for: vital statistics. All vital statistics—including birth, marriage, and death certificates—filed after October 1, 1874 (the date registry offices [*Standesämter*] were introduced in Prussia), are stored locally in the relevant district registry office. Berlin currently has some 22 districts; for phone numbers, check in the front of the Berlin Yellow Pages, in the *Bürgerservice* section, under *Bezirksämter* (district offices).

The following archives and libraries in the city may be of help:

Stiftung Neue Synagoge Berlin—Centrum Judaicum Archiv (New Synagogue Berlin—Centrum Judaicum Foundation Archive)
Oranienburger Strasse 28-30 (tel: 284 01225). **Transportation:** *U-Bahn line U6 to Oranienburger Tor or S-Bahn line S1, S2, or S25 to Oranienburger Strasse; Bus 157 to Oranienburger Strasse; Tram 1 or 13 to Oranienburger Strasse;* **Open:** *Tuesday–Thursday 9am–4pm.*

This archive contains a great many documents and records on German Jewish history, but for family researchers resources are somewhat limited. This is not a library where you can sit down and browse: prior appointments are necessary to use the archive. Those interested in researching family from Berlin may find the following resources in the Centrum Judaicum archive especially helpful:

A register of voting members of the Jewish Community for the years 1883, 1886, 1892, 1898, 1904, 1907, 1910, and 1913 is contained in *Verzeichnisse der wahlfähigen Mitglieder der Jüdischen Gemeinde zu Berlin* (Register of the Voting Members of the Jewish Community of Berlin);

An index of people relinquishing their membership in the Jewish

Community organization for the periods 1873 to circa 1941 and after 1945;

An index of those persecuted for "racial" reasons by the Nazis who applied after the war for recognition as "Victims of Fascism." The records are known as *OdF-Kartei* (Victims of Fascism index);

A register of Jewish Community members immediately after 1945.

Due to the stringent German laws concerning the protection of data, some of these resources cannot be viewed personally. Questions, with the most accurate names and information possible, can be submitted in writing or in person by appointment.

The New Synagogue archive also contains documents of the General Archive of the German Jews and material, dating from the end of the eighteenth century to the beginning of the twentieth century, from some 400 German-Jewish communities and organizations. There are, however, virtually no vital statistics records among them.

Jüdische Gemeinde Bibliothek
(Jewish Community Library)

Main branch: Fasanenstr. 79-80 (tel: 880 28235). **Transportation:** *U-Bahn line U2 or U9 to Zoologischer Garten or U15 to Uhlandstrasse; S-Bahn line S3, S5, S7 or S9 to Zoologischer Garten; Bus 109, 119, 129 or 219 to Uhlandstrasse;* **Open:** *Monday–Thursday 11am–8pm, Friday 11am–3pm.*

Subsidiary branch: Oranienburger Str. 28 (tel: 284 01227). **Transportation:** *U-Bahn line U6 to Oranienburger Tor; S-Bahn line S1 or S2 to Oranienburger Strasse; Tram 1 or 13 to Oranienburger Strasse;* **Open:** *Monday 10am-noon & 1pm–6:30pm and Thursday 10am–noon & 1pm–4pm.*

In addition to an excellent collection of general works on German-Jewish history, the Jewish community library has the following resources, all of which can be viewed comfortably in the library without prior appointment:

Listings of Berlin Jewish citizens from 1791–1851, which is contained in *Judenbürgerbücher der Stadt Berlin 1809–1851, mit Ergänzungen für die Jahre 1791–1809* (Jewish Citizens Books for Berlin 1809–51, with a supplement for the years 1791–1809);

Listings of Jewish marriages in Berlin for the years 1723–1813, contained in *Jüdische Trauungen in Berlin 1759–1813, mit Ergänzungen für die Jahre von 1723–1759* (Jewish Marriages in Berlin 1759–1813, with a supplement for the years from 1723–59);

Names and addresses of Jewish Berliners for the years 1929/30 and 1931, contained in *Jüdisches Adressbuch für Gross-Berlin* (Jewish Address Book for Greater Berlin);

Catalogs of the names of Nazi victims, available in a volume that covers Berlin alone—*Gedenkbuch Berlins der jüdischen Opfer des Nationalsozialismus* (Berlin Memorial Book for the Jewish Victims of National Socialism), and an older volume, which unfortunately includes numerous errors, for Berlin and the former West German states—*Gedenkbuch für die Opfer der Verfolgung der Juden unter der nationalsozialistischen Gewaltherrschaft in Deutschland 1933–1945* (Memorial Book for the Victims of the Persecution of the Jews under National Socialist Tyranny 1933–45);

A listing of over 10,000 Jewish soldiers killed in World War I, contained in *Die jüdischen Gefallenen—Ein Gedenkbuch* (The Jewish Fallen—A Memorial Book).

The library contains a number of other valuable resources, including a complete collection of the yearbooks of the Leo Baeck Institute, which is dedicated to German-Jewish history. The articles in the yearbooks are not genealogically oriented, but they are often quite detailed and most of them are in English.

There's also a good selection of books on local Jewish history, usually produced by district administrations and varying in quality. Nearly all are in German.

Zentrum für Berlin-Studien
(Center for Berlin Studies)

Breite Strasse 36 (tel: 902 26485). **Transportation:** *Bus 147 or 257 to Mühlendamm/Breite Strasse;* **Open:** *Monday–Friday 10am–7pm, Saturday 1pm–6pm.*

Located in the historic Ribbeck Haus, a seventeenth-century mansion and a rare survivor of wartime bombing, this library is dedicated to Berlin and contains a great deal of information about all aspects of the city, including the Jewish community and its destruction. Almost all the material is in German, but the librarians are helpful and speak English.

The Center has copies of many of the large source books available at the Jewish Community Library—Jewish Citizens Books for Berlin; Jewish Marriages in Berlin; Jewish Address Books; and the Memorial Books—as well as general Berlin address books that go back to 1799 and telephone books that go back to 1913.

Several other sources, somewhat scattered, may be useful:

The Weissensee Cemetery *(Herbert-Baum-Strasse 45; tel: 925 3330)* has a complete list of burials on the grounds from 1880 to the present. These index cards include date of birth, date of death, and location of grave. Files with additional information about funeral announcements and relatives are also available here, as is an incomplete list of burials in the Schönhauser Allee cemetery.

Deportation lists, along with files relating to property confiscations before deportation and from emigrants, are located in the **Landesarchiv Berlin (Berlin State Archive),** *Kalckreuthstr. 1-2 (tel: 2123 2182).* This archive also contains records from the Berlin Municipal Court on "Jews and Dissidents" for the years 1847–74 and microfilms of some documents of the Berlin Jewish Community. Historic maps of Berlin are available for sale here as well.

An index for the census of May 17, 1939 (*Ergänzungskarten der Volkszählung vom 17.5.1939*) can be found in the **Bundesarchiv (Federal Archive),** *Finckensteinalle 63 (tel: 843 500).*

The world's greatest genealogists, the Mormons, have a genealogy center in Berlin that may be of use. **The Mormon Church and Genealogical Center** is located at *Klingelhoffer Strasse 24 (262 1089)* and is open Wed–Fri from 4pm–9pm and Sat 8am–1pm.

An essential resource for burrowers into Jewish-German genealogy is *Stammbaum*, a periodical devoted wholly to the subject. Contact:

> **Stammbaum**
> *Frank Mecklenburg*
> *Leo Baeck Institute*
> *29 E 73rd St*
> *New York, NY 10021*
> *(212) 744 6400*
> *e-mail: frank@lbi.com*

PROPERTY CLAIMS

Making a claim for property confiscated or compulsorily sold during the Third Reich will almost assuredly be a long, time-consuming and unpleasant experience. Make sure you have the time and the fortitude. Assemble as many documents as possible and contact a good lawyer.

The government deadlines for making such claims have long since passed: in West Germany not long after the war and in the former communist German Democratic Republic in 1992. However, there remains a possibility to have lost property, at least any located in the former East Germany, returned even if a onetime property owner has not yet filed.

The Conference on Jewish Claims against Germany, an organization established in 1951 and usually referred to simply as "the Claims Conference," has made claims on almost all unclaimed Jewish properties. If the property you are seeking is among that now claimed by the organization, you can pursue your petition through the Claims Conference. Contact:

Conference on Jewish Claims against Germany
Sophienstrasse 26
D-60487 Frankfurt-am-Main
Tel: (069) 970 7080
Fax: (069) 970 70811

There is also a Berlin office at *Uferstrasse 6 (283 0530)*, although they will probably refer you to the Frankfurt office.

For the record, the appropriate German government office for reparations and restitution for Nazi crimes is:

Zentrale Auskunftsstelle zur Wiedergutmachung national-sozialstischen Unrechts
(Central Information Office for the Reparation of National Socialist Injustices)
Riehler Platz 2
Postfach 14 01 40
50491 Köln (tel: 0221 977 80)

11 | A Walking Tour through Mitte

This tour attempts, with the help of old buildings, memorials, and sometimes just empty spaces, to evoke a portrait of Jewish life in Berlin from its beginnings to the nineteenth century. It was during these years that the Jewish community of Berlin rose from obscurity to become one of Europe's leading centers of Jewish thought and achievement.

The tour starts in the environs of the oldest part of Berlin and ends up traipsing through what is now becoming increasingly known, especially in guidebooks and tourist brochures, as the "Jewish Quarter." The name is a misnomer. Although the neighborhood was the site of much early Jewish settlement, and became a favored destination for Yiddish-speaking eastern European Jewish émigrés around the turn of the century, in truth Jews were sprinkled liberally throughout the city, and the Jewish population in this area at no time exceeded about 10%. What lent the district its reputation was a concentration of Orthodox and Chasidic Jewish immigrants from eastern Europe, conspicuous in their black coats and hats, who arrived between the 1880s and 1920s.

■ Hand-held Walking Tours

Jewish life and history form a favorite topic for many of the city's walking tour services, and you can find groups tramping through the Sheunenviertel on just about any day of the week. Most of these tours are conducted in German, but many companies can provide English-language tours. Try StattReisen Berlin (455 3028; they also conduct tours with Jewish content to Vilna, Cracow, Lublin, and other destinations in eastern Europe), Berlin Tourismus Marketing (264 74853) or check one of the city program magazines (Tip, Zitty, or Berlin Programm) for other tour companies.

A good bet for English speakers is Berlin Walks, which conducts lively and well-informed tours led by native English speakers. Of particular interest are "Jewish Life in Berlin" and "Infamous Third Reich Sites." For more information, call 301 9194.

However, it's also true that many sites of great importance for the community were located here, and a walk through the neighborhood reveals a rich Jewish heritage.

Like all such tours, the walk's course is determined more by geography than historical progression, and there are inevitable skips and jumps in time. What you may lose in strict chronology, though, you will gain in a heightened sense of history.

Walking Time: Approximately 2 1/2 hours.
Starting Point: Klosterstrasse U-Bahn station.
End Point: The Neue Synagoge (New Synagogue).
Nearest transportation to end point: Oranienburger Tor U-Bahn
station and Oranienburger Strasse S-Bahn station.

*Take U-Bahn line U2 to Klosterstrasse and leave by the
Grunerstrasse exit. Directly in front of you is the* Fernsehturm *(TV
Tower), built by the East German government in the late 1960s and
now a cherished Berlin landmark. Walk toward it to Grunerstrasse,
turn left, and walk about a block to the first cross street:
Jüdenstrasse—Jews' Street.*

❶ Of the very earliest presence of Jews in Berlin, nothing physical remains except a name: Jews' Street. It is one of the oldest

extant Berlin street names, dating from sometime around the end of the thirteenth century. At that time, the homes of the few Jewish traders and merchants were confined to a single courtyard, called the *Grosser Judenhof* (Greater Jews' Court), and eventually the street on which the court lay became known as Jews' Street. The street continues on the other side of Grunerstrasse as well, passing to the right of the Rotes Rathaus, the city hall, which is the large red brick building with the Italian Renaissance tower.

Berlin's first Jews were involved mainly in trading, money changing, and money lending. A handful were connected to the royal court as bankers and jewelers, but most were dirt poor. They enjoyed neither economic nor residential security, and were frequently expelled from the city: in 1349 – 50, when blamed for the "Black Death" bubonic plague, in 1446, in 1510, when they were accused of desecrating a host, and again in 1571. These expulsions were often accompanied by rioting and murder.

Continue another block to the next intersection, cross Stralauer Strasse, then turn right and cross Mühlendamm. Turn left up Mühlendamm. About half a block further is the Ephraimpalais (Ephraim Palace), the gold-balconied building on your right.

❷ The Ephraimpalais, considered the finest example of Baroque architecture in the city when it was built, was the home of Veitel Heine Ephraim (1703–75), a banker and minter for King Frederick II and a leading member of the Jewish community. The house, completed in 1765, was designed by Friedrich Wilhelm Dietrichs, who also designed the Operncafe (originally built as a mansion for the Prussian finance minister) on Unter den Linden.

Ephraim was in many respects a typical court Jew, providing loans and economic guidance to the ruler in exchange for special protection. In 1745 he was appointed court jeweler to Frederick the Great and soon became involved in banking activities on behalf of the Hohenzollern ruler.

During the Seven Years' War (known in the United States as the French and Indian War), 1756–63, Ephraim and another court banker, Daniel Itzig, were given government contracts to finance the conflict by issuing debased coins (which became known, derisively, as "Ephraimiten.") Though this inflationary measure helped Frederick II defray war costs, it impoverished much of the merchant class, and the ensuing public outcry cost Ephraim his job. The low silver content of the coins that bore his name was not, however, Ephraim's doing: the amount of silver in each piece was strictly regulated by the government.

For a quarter of a century, from 1749 to 1775, Ephraim was head of the Berlin Jewish Community. In this position, as in his office as court jeweler, he followed in the footsteps of his father Heine (Chaim) Ephraim (1665–1748).

Like so many other "old" buildings in Berlin, the Ephraimpalais is a reconstruction. In 1935, Mühlendamm, the street outside, was widened, and the original mansion was torn down. But pieces of the facade were saved, carefully boxed and numbered, and survived the war. When the East German government undertook the restoration of this area for the city's 750th birthday in 1987, the West German government unpacked and donated the original facade.

The interior (which once featured Ephraim's private synagogue) houses a modest museum with an exhibition of Berlin art and artists and a collection of coins, including examples of the infamous "Ephraimiten."

Walk down the stairs to the right of the entrance and into the Nikolaiviertel, the re-created core of old Berlin. A few feet along Probststrasse, on your right, is the Knoblauchhaus, which has a small connection to Jewish history in the city. One member of this prominent gentile Berlin family, architect Eduard Knoblauch, designed the New Synagogue on Oranienburger Strasse. Continue past the house and you'll enter the central square of the quarter, dominated by the Nikolaikirche, again a reconstruction of an original destroyed by wartime bombing. Inside is an exhibition with some history of the church and artifacts from the original, mostly carved tombstones. Skirt around the right side of the church to the Lessing Haus at Nikolaikirchplatz 7.

❸ So little survives of pre-war Berlin, and particularly of pre-war Jewish Berlin, that some liberties must be taken in a walking tour. To discuss Moses Mendelssohn is essential; however, not a single Mendelssohn artifact—home or workplace or bed—remains extant. The best that can be done is to stop at the house (re-constructed, of course) of his best friend, writer Gotthold Ephraim Lessing, a place that Mendelssohn visited many times.

The plaque above the entrance reads: "Here stood the house in which Lessing finished [his play] 'Minna von Barnhelm' in 1765. The City of Berlin, 1913."

Moses Mendelssohn was the most famous, influential and respected Jew of his time, a major figure of the German Enlightenment, initiator of the Jewish Haskalah (Enlightenment) movement, and one of the towering intellectual figures in the country.

He was born in Dessau in 1729, the son of an impoverished Torah scribe. He became a pupil of Rabbi David Fraenkel as a young boy, and when his mentor moved to Berlin to become rabbi at the Heidereutergasse Synagogue, the fourteen-year-old Mendelssohn followed him.

In Berlin he became exposed for the first time to the world of non-Jewish scholarship, and he quickly mastered the tools— including Latin, Greek, French, geometry, and logic—necessary to pursue his new-found passion for learning.

In 1754 Mendelssohn met the young writer and philosopher Gotthold Lessing. This was the beginning of a lifelong friendship and working relationship that eventually produced Lessing's great play, *Nathan the Wise*, whose title character was based on Mendelssohn.

Lessing was instrumental in launching Mendelssohn's philosophical career. He took a manuscript of Mendelssohn's jottings and had them published without the author's knowledge— evidently the first book by a Jew in the German language. Mendelssohn went on to write several other major works of Enlightenment philosophy, produced a German translation of the Torah, and also published a Hebrew-language magazine.

On January 4, 1786, Mendelssohn, fifty-seven years old, died. Berlin's Jewish shops and offices closed for two days.

Circle to the opposite side of the church and exit through the small street Am Nussbaum. Turn left onto the next street, Spandauer Strasse. Continue up the street to the next intersection, cross Spandauer Strasse, and continue in the same direction to the front of the Rotes Rathaus (Red City Hall), built in 1859 and still in use as the headquarters for the city administration. Head away from the entrance, past the Neptunebrunnen (Neptune Fountain)—a playful acquatic sculpture from 1891—and beyond it to the Marienkirche (St. Mary's Church).

❹ What is now the relatively spacious plaza you've just walked through was once part of the crooked and cramped heart of medieval Berlin. In front of the Marienkirche, whose origins date back to 1270, was a small patch of open ground called the New Market, used by stall keepers for selling produce and, not incidentally, by the authorities for public executions. Two infamous executions held here have a place on this tour: the burning at the stake of 38 Jews in 1510 on charges of desecrating a host and the execution of the court Jew Lippold in 1573.

The 1510 case followed the familiar script of such trials. In that year Jews were accused of desecrating a Host and stealing sacred objects from a village church near Berlin. One hundred and eleven Jews were rounded up and arrested, 51 of these were sentenced to death and 38 executed on this site. In 1539, the Protestant reformer Melanchthon proved that the evidence against the Jews had been faked.

A memorial plaque honoring those victims now stands in a small yard behind an apartment house at Mollstrasse 11, southeast of Alexanderplatz, the site traditionally thought to be their place of burial.

A half century later this site was the setting for the execution of the small community's most prominent member, Lippold. He was the "supervisor" of the Jews of the Brandenburg province when Elector Joachim II of Brandenburg (1535–71) appointed him royal mintmaster and financier in 1565. Despite, or perhaps because of, the fact that monarch and minter were confidants, Lippold was unpopular with the rest of the court, as well as, evidently, other Jews. When Joachim died, on January 3, 1571, his successor, Elector John George, had Lippold arrested for embezzlement and theft. Subsequently, the charge of murdering Joachim by poison was added. But, after an investigation failed to turn up any evidence, Lippold was freed.

Two years later, investigators doggedly pursuing the case turned up a kabbalistic book in his possession. They considering the tome an obvious sign of sorcery, and Lippold was rearrested and tortured until he confessed. He admitted working with the devil, dispensing love potions, manufacturing a magic key that opened any lock, and using sorcery to win over Joachim.

Lippold was put on trial on January 28, 1573. He was evidently offered a commutation of the death sentence if he converted to

Christianity but this reprieve he refused.

On this spot, in front of a large crowd, he was again tortured and then executed, drawn and quartered, and his bowels burned. After this gruesome spectacle, the city's Jews were attacked and their property burned. They were then driven out of Brandenburg, and the province remained without Jews for another century until the arrival in 1671, at the invitation of the king, of 50 families from Vienna. This event is considered the genesis of Berlin's modern Jewish community.

Cross Karl-Liebknecht-Strasse at the intersection west of the church, then turn right and walk back toward the church until you reach Rosenstrasse, which forms a passageway on your left through the shopping strip. Walk to the small square beyond, the site of Berlin's first synagogue, the Heidereutergasse or Alte (old) Synagogue.

❺ When the 50 families that formed the kernel of the modern Jewish community in Berlin were admitted to the city in 1671, it was expressly forbidden for them to erect a synagogue. For many years they made do with private dwellings and small rooms for services. In 1712 permission was finally granted to erect a public synagogue and the Baroque structure, designed by Michael Kemmeter, was dedicated on September 7, 1714. It was prominent enough to attract a visit by King Friedrich Wilhelm I, with his son, the future Frederick the Great, in tow, four years later.

The interior of the Great Synagogue, as it was known at the time, was considered one of the most impressive in the German-speaking lands, and one observer compared it favorably with the famous Portugese synagogue in Amsterdam, built some 40 years previously. The building, set off from the street by a large courtyard, featured high arched windows and a peaked roof, but was purposely inconspicuous and without towers or domes.

A large floridly carved Baroque ark dominated the interior, which was decorated throughout with carved woodwork. The parochet —the curtain hanging in front of the ark—was a gift from King Friedrich Wilhelm I. Women were seated in two balconies, one above the other, in the rear over the entrance.

Here Mendelssohn's mentor, Rabbi David Fraenkel, led a congregation that included Mendelssohn, Marcus Herz, David

Friedländer, and other early luminaries of the Jewish community.

By the early nineteenth century, the synagogue was too small for the growing community, and, after much debate between Orthodox and Liberal wings, major renovations were carried out in 1856 by Eduard Knoblauch, who not long after would design the New Synagogue on Oranienberger Strasse. He gutted the Baroque structure and replaced the interior with classical elements.

After the construction in 1866 of the large New Synagogue on Oranienburger Strasse, this building, until then known as the Great Synagogue, became known as the Old Synagogue. It declined in importance, but continued to serve the community. Due to its location next to a post office, the Old Synagogue was not damaged during the Kristallnacht pogrom. However, during the course of the war it was destroyed by Allied bombing.

The sculpture that now occupies the small square commemorates a striking but relatively unknown incident that took place here, the Rosenstrasse Women's Protest, the single known instance of mass public protest against the treatment of Jews during the Nazi regime.

❻ The fury of Nazi anti-Semitism was brought to bear against Jews almost immediately after Hitler came to power on January 30, 1933, but, because of the peculiarities (and absurdities) of Nazi "racial" definitions, not all Jews were affected to the same degree. Even until well into the war, many Berlin Jews in mixed marriages were awarded a kind of protected status and were not subject to deportation by the Nazi government. In Berlin this exemption came to an abrupt end on February 28, 1943 when the SS conducted the so-called *Fabrik-Aktion* (Factory Action), rounding up some 1,500 to 2,500 Jewish men and youths at their places of work in preparation for deportation to Auschwitz. The detainees were held here in an administration building of the Jewish Community that had been taken over by the SS.

The next day, as word spread of where these prisoners were held, a group of their non-Jewish wives spontaneously assembled in front of the building. Over the next five days and nights, the crowd of women grew to several hundred, and perhaps over a thousand, calling loudly for the release of their families, confronting the SS with cries of "Give us our men back" and "Murderers!" and several times facing down machine guns set up by the Nazis.

The SS, panicked by this unprecedented protest, finally opened the doors and released the prisoners. Amazingly, 25 men already sent to Auschwitz were actually brought back to Berlin and released.

The demonstration, relatively obscure until recently, is commemorated by this stone monument, *Block der Frauen* (Block of Women), produced by Ingeborg Hunzinger in 1995. Human figures and Jewish symbols play over the stones, which form a semi-circle around the central figures of two mourning and protesting women. The inscriptions on the rear of the monument state: "1943: The strength of civil disobedience, the vigor of love overcomes the violence of dictatorship; Give us our men back; Women were standing here, defeating death; Jewish men were free."

Continue on Rosenstrasse until you reach An der Spandauer Brücke. Turn right and follow the road as it passes underneath the S-Bahn train tracks. Keep along the road as it crosses Rosenthaler Strasse and veers to your left onto Oranienburger Strasse. Continue for a block and take the next right on Grosse Hamburger Strasse. Continue for a dozen or so yards to the small plaza on your right. Walk into the grassy park.

❼ This is the site of the first cemetery of Berlin's modern Jewish community, dedicated in 1672 and destroyed by the Nazis in 1943. The plot is now well-groomed and light, and it is hard to imagine that it once contained an overgrown, ivy-tangled graveyard. Only the quiet serenity remains the same. For 150 years this was the community's only cemetery, and all its dead, from the powerful to the pauper, were buried here.

The most illustrious resident of the old cemetery was Moses Mendelssohn (1729–86), whom we've already encountered. His original stone was among those destroyed in 1943; the present marker, placed at the presumed site of his grave, dates from 1990. It is the single gravestone standing now, though fragments of some of the other stones have been installed by the west and south walls.

Veitel Heine Ephraim (1703–75), whom we have also already encountered on this tour, was buried here as well. Other prominent Berlin figures laid to rest here included:

Daniel Itzig (1723–99), a banker, entrepreneur and leading figure in the Jewish community. He worked with Veitel Ephraim on government contracts during the Seven Years' War and later became court banker and financial advisor to the crown. He was appointed chief representative for Prussian Jewry by Frederick II and worked hard to improve the rights and conditions of the Jewish community.

David Fraenkel (1707–62), most famous as Moses Mendelssohn's mentor, but a prominent talmudic scholar in his own right. He was chief rabbi of Berlin from 1743 until his death and wrote a well-received commentary on the Palestinian Talmud that revived interest in that previously neglected text.

Marcus Herz (1747–1803), one of Berlin's most distinguished figures. He was a pupil and confidant of the philosopher Immanuel Kant, served as physician-in-chief at Berlin's Jewish Hospital, agitated for Jewish civil rights, and wrote many medical, philosophical, and theological works. He has been overshadowed not only by his friend Mendelssohn, but also by his wife, Henrietta Herz, popular hostess of one of Berlin's celebrated literary salons. She later converted and is buried in a Christian cemetery at Hallesches Tor.

A plaque affixed to the southern wall inside the grounds commemorates the lost cemetery:

"In memory of the oldest burial place of Berlin's Jewish community, in use from 1672 to 1827 and destroyed on the orders of the Gestapo."

In 1943 the Nazis laid the cemetery to waste when they dug a bomb trench through the plot and reinforced it with gravestones. After the German surrender, the site was used as a mass grave for war casualties, mostly German civilians and soldiers. They are memorialized with a small stone plaque on the east wall of the site. It states: "In 1945, countless victims of the war were buried in this old cemetery of the Jewish community."

Prior to the Second World War, the grounds were shielded from the street by a Jewish Home for the Aged. This home was taken over by the Nazis in 1941 and used as a collection point and detention center for the deportation of Berlin Jews to Theresienstadt and Auschwitz. The ruined cemetery was put to use by SS guards as an exercise yard for the Jewish prisoners. The home was destroyed in 1945.

The sculptural group to the left of the entrance was installed in 1985 to commemorate the tens of thousands of Jews who passed through the old age home before deportation. The 13 haunted female figures, by Will Lammert, were created in 1957 and originally intended for a memorial at Ravensbrück concentration camp. To the left of the figures is a memorial tablet that reads: "On this site stood the first old-age home of Berlin's Jewish community, transformed by the Gestapo in 1942 into a collection camp for Jewish citizens. 55,000 Berlin Jews from infants to the elderly were shipped to Auschwitz and Theresienstadt concentration camps and bestially murdered. Never forget it; prevent war; safeguard peace."

Keep walking along Grosse Hamburger Strasse. The next building, at number 27, is the Oberschule (secondary school) of the Jewish Community, a school with a long and noble pedigree.

❽ Inspired by the ideas of Moses Mendelssohn, two colleagues of the Haskalah philosopher, David Friedländer and Daniel Itzig, founded a Jewish Free School in 1778. It was the first school in Germany to combine religious instruction with a secular education. Intended to prepare students for a business career, it included such subjects as arithmetic, bookkeeping, German and French, in addition to religious tutoring and Hebrew-language instruction. Until 1819, when it was forbidden by government decree, non-Jews were included in the faculty and student body.

Always in financial straits, the school was taken over by the Jewish Community in 1826, and in 1863 it moved to this location. The present building was erected in 1905-06. The architect was Johann Höniger, designer of the orthodox Adass Yisroel synagogue on Tucholsky Strasse and the liberal synagogues on Rykestrasse and Levetzowstrasse. The inscription "Knabenschule der Juedischen Gemeinde" (Jewish Community Boys' School) can still be read over the entrance.

Schooling for girls lagged behind. The first girls' school, emphasizing household skills, was founded by the Community in 1835. In 1931, it joined the boys' school in this building.

On June 30, 1942, the school, along with all other Jewish educational institutions, was closed by the German government. The building was empty for many years and eventually became a vocational school.

With the reunification of the country, the building reverted to Jewish Community ownership and on August 6, 1993, some 50 years after it had closed, a Jewish high school once again opened here.

A plaque (by Gerhard Thieme) installed on the facade in 1983 features a profile in relief of Mendelssohn and this inscription: "'Search for truth, love beauty, desire good, do the best.' Moses Mendelssohn, philosopher and friend of Lessing's. Founder of the first Jewish School in Berlin. Born on September 6, 1729 in Dessau. Died on January 4, 1768 in Berlin."

Cross the street and almost directly opposite the school you'll see a yard behind a wooden fence. Open the gate and walk in.

❾ This lot was once an apartment building, destroyed by wartime bombing in February 1945. The names of former tenants, their occupations, and the years of their tenancy are displayed on large plaques affixed to the walls on either side.

This is an art piece, entitled "The Missing House," created by Christian Boltanski, a French artist. It was installed during an international art exhibition in 1990 and intended at the time to be temporary. But the piece proved so popular that it was decided to keep the plaques up.

It is a simple but powerful piece. Here, "The Missing House" suggests, neighbors of various classes—white collar workers, truck drivers, clerks—and religions—J. Schnapp, noted on the north wall, was Jewish; G. Jacoby, listed on the south wall, had a Jewish father —got along. The work reminds us not only of the lives disrupted, but of a community destroyed. The contrast of the present silent emptiness with a reminder of the former workaday activity is compelling and continues to make Boltanski's piece a popular one.

Continue on Grosse Hamburger Strasse for two blocks. Turn right onto Auguststrasse and walk to Gipsstrasse. Bear right onto Gipsstrasse and continue to number 3, just around the corner. Note the plaque on the facade.

❿ The East German-vintage plaque here reads: "In this house resistance fighters of the Baum Group lived. Sala Kochmann, executed by the Fascists in Plötzensee on August 18, 1942. Martin Kochmann, executed by the Fascists in September, 1943. Their struggle is also our struggle! The dead admonish us!"

The Herbert Baum Group, the best known German Jewish resistance group, is notable for a number of reasons. This communist resistance cell, almost exclusively Jewish, was one of the few groups in Germany to go beyond mere organizing and leafleting to direct action. Their arson attack on a Nazi propaganda exhibit , now commemorated by a memorial in the Lustgarten, was one of the most notable—even if futile—actions of the underground struggle against the Nazi state.

In early 1942, Nazi leader Joseph Goebbels set up an anti-communist propaganda exhibit entitled "The Soviet Paradise" in a temporary structure in the Lustgarten on Unter den Linden. In addition to its depictions of "unbearable" life under communism, it contained anti-Semitic slander.

The Baum group decided to burn down the exhibit. After elaborate planning, on May 18, 1942, several members entered the exhibit and set off incendiary devices. The flames were quickly extinguished, however, and in a matter of days most members of the Baum Group were arrested. Although unsuccessful in its immediate objective, it did become the first example of resistance in Germany to be mentioned in the U.S. press: the New York Times carried a front-page article on the ". . . Bomb Plot at Anti-Red Exhibit."

The Kochmanns were, along with Herbert and Marianne Baum, initiators of the resistance group. The apartment here was used as a regular meeting place for them, and it was from here that the group left to carry out their arson attack on the "Soviet Paradise" exhibit.

This building also housed a Jewish kindergarten where two other members of the Baum group, Marianne Joachim and Hanni Meyer, worked.

Go back to Grosse Hamburger Strasse and continue in the same direction as before. Another block up and you'll find a park, Koppenplatz. Continue to the far side and you'll find a small and unusual sculpture – a bronze table and chairs – officially called the Denkmal für das Wirken jüdischer Bürger in Berlin *(Memorial to the Contributions of the Jewish Citizens of Berlin).*

⓫ For the 50th anniversary of the Kristallnacht pogrom in 1988, the East German government called for a competition to commemorate the former Jewish residents of the city—the first large memorial dedicated in the German Democratic Republic to Berlin's Jews.

The memorial, cast in bronze, is a wall-less representation of a room, consisting of only a parquet floor, a table and two chairs. One chair lies knocked over on the floor, a symbol of abrupt and forced departure. The stark sculpture, unusual for an "official" piece of communist public art, is by Karl Biedermann.

The perimeter of the floor is framed by lines from Nelly Sachs, the Jewish poet who shared the 1966 Nobel Prize for Literature with S. Y. Agnon: "Oh, the dwelling places of death,/Invitingly prepared/For the house's host, who was otherwise a guest-/Oh, you fingers,/The threshhold laying/Like a knife between life and death-//Oh, you chimneys,/Oh, you fingers,/and Israel's body through the air in smoke!" Nelly Sachs (December 10, 1891 Berlin—May 12, 1970 Stockholm).

Turn left on Linienstrasse and walk down a couple of blocks to number 154a, where another old East German plaque commemorates a resistance figure, Margarete Kaufmann.

⑫ After a political initiation with the Poale Zion (Workers of Zion) socialist Zionist group, Margarete Kaufmann became a member of the Communist Party in 1932. In the early years of the Third Reich she wrote for several underground newspapers and carried out anti-Nazi work in central and southern Berlin. She was arrested in 1938 and sentenced to 15 years in prison. In 1942, however, she was handed over to the SS and murdered in Auschwitz. The plaque reads: "The dead admonish. In this house lived the resistance fighter Margarete Kaufmann, born June 18, 1908, murdered by the Fascists."

You may have noted already that neither this old East German plaque nor that for Sala and Martin Kochmann of the Baum Group mention that those commemorated were Jewish. In the strict ideology of the German Democratic Republic, meaningful resistance to the Nazis came only from the Communist Party, and resistance from Jews—who, as neither a political grouping nor an economic class, did not fit well into a Marxist framework—was not recognized as having any special significance.

Both Margarete Kaufmann and the Herbert Baum Group were communist (they would not have rated a plaque otherwise), but the fact that they were Jewish most certainly had an effect on their thinking and the conduct of their resistance.

Continue up the street to the next corner and turn left. Stop at the courtyard gate at Tucholskystrasse 40, just before the Beth Café. This is the location of the synagogue and administrative offices of the orthodox Adass Yisroel congregation.

⓭ The first thing you'll notice, no doubt, is the policeman on guard here. Jewish offices, and synagogues during services, always have police on hand. For Americans and Britons, this is more unsettling than reassuring. It is, unfortunately, routine in many European countries.

Peer through the gate and you'll see a second portal topped by an arch with a Star of David. The original entrance to the Adass Yisroel Synagogue, this is a rare survivor of the Third Reich.

The embrace of modernity initiated by Moses Mendelssohn and his followers resulted in a century of creeping liberalization in the unitary congregation of Berlin. The strains long present in the Community reached the breaking point in 1869, when a group of Orthodox members broke away and established the Adass Yisroel Congregation as a self-described *gesetztreu* (faithful to Jewish law) group.

For a religious leader, they turned to Esriel Hildesheimer, an energetic scholar and educator with a widespread reputation as a champion of strict Orthodoxy. He was, along with the famous Samuel Raphael Hirsch, a leader of the neo-Orthodox movement in Germany, which, although it accepted interaction with the modern secular world, brooked no changes in Halachah. Hildesheimer could be strident in his condemnation of the non-Orthodox, but unlike Hirsch, he advocated cooperation among all tendencies within Judaism, particularly in the fight against anti-Semitism.

In 1873, Hildesheimer established the *Rabbinerseminar zu Berlin* (The Rabbinical Seminary of Berlin), the first modern Orthodox rabbinical seminary in Germany. Hildesheimer's school was created as an alternative to Germany's other two rabbinical seminaries, both of which were liberal. They questioned the divine origin of the Torah, a blasphemy that for Hildesheimer put them beyond the pale of true Judaism.

Ironically, when Adass Yisroel was relocated here in 1904 by Hildesheimer's son, Meyer, the Rabbinical Seminary ended up on the same street as the College for the Science of Judaism (discussed below), the most liberal of Germany's other two seminaries and an institution that Hildesheimer despised.

The Adass Yisroel Synagogue, a boys' school, and administrative offices were also located here. The synagogue, tucked deep within a second, inner courtyard, survived the Kristallnacht pogrom, but was destroyed during a bombing raid in the war. The remains were torn down in 1967.

The Adass Yisroel congregation did not survive the Nazi terror. The organization, which at the beginning of the 1930s counted about a sixth of Berlin Jews as members, was dissolved by the German government in December 1939.

In 1985, Adass Yisroel was reestablished in Berlin, and a new synagogue was dedicated in 1990. The following year the affiliated kosher Beth Café opened next door, and in 1992, Kolbo, a store offering kosher foodstuffs, ritual objects and Jewish books and recordings, was established around the corner at Auguststrasse 77/78.

Walk to the end of the block and take a left on Auguststrasse. Stop in front of Auguststrasse 14-15, on the right side of the street.

🄬 As early as 1756, the Jewish Community established its own hospital. Originally located on Oranienburger Strasse, the hospital was relocated to this building, built by Eduard Knoblauch, who also designed the New Synagogue, in 1861. For almost 50 years, until 1914, it served as the Jewish Hospital until the institution was moved again, this time to more a more spacious building on Iranischen Strasse, in the Wedding district, where it still stands (though it is no longer affiliated with the Community).

Following the relocation of the hospital, this building was used over the next 30 years as home base for several social and cultural institutions, including a kindergarten, dental clinic, a cooking school, the *Chevra Kadischa* (burial society), and a home for refugee children from eastern Europe that was later opened to other children from troubled or underprivileged environments.

In 1942, the rear building was turned into a collection point by the Nazis for deportations.

Go through the central passage to the inner courtyard. To the left of the entrance to the back building, which now serves as a public school, is a plaque with the following inscription:

"This house, built by the architect Eduard Knoblauch, was financed and maintained by the donations of Berlin Jews. From 1861–1914 it was the hospital of the Jewish Community. After the First World War, Jewish refugee children from eastern Europe found a home here called Ahavah (love).

From 1941–43 this house was a collection point in which elderly Jews waited for their transport to death. Fifty years after the deportations we remember with this plaque the forgotten occupants of this house. November 1992. The Berlin Active Museum of Fascism and Resistance."

⑮ The structure next door to the front building, Auguststrasse 11-13, a Bauhaus-influenced brick structure by Alexander Beer, was also once part of the Jewish Community's social system: Built in 1930, it housed a Jewish girls' school. Like all other Jewish schools in Germany, this was closed by the government on June 30, 1942.

Return to Tucholskystrasse, turn left and cross Oranienburger Strasse. About 2 blocks down on the right side of the street, at Tucholskystrasse 9, is the building that once housed the Hochschule für die Wissenschaft des Judentums *(College for the Science of Judaism)*.

⑯ One of the groups that helped to modernize Judaism in the nineteenth century was the "Science of Judaism" movement. This academic school applied modern techniques of scholarship to investigate Jewish history in an attempt to discover the origins of practices and beliefs, and place the religion in historical perspective. It had a powerful role in modernizing Jewish thought and ritual and was hugely influential in the development of the Reform and Conservative branches of Judaism.

The leaders of the movement had long seen a need for a school to teach its methodology and perspective, and after many years of discussion and several attempts, an academy was established in 1872. Originally located on Unter den Linden, it relocated here, in its own building, in 1907. The College for the Science of Judaism soon became an important center for Judaic studies and developed into a seminary to train rabbis and teachers. Nonrabbinical students were, however, welcome, and women were admitted as well. Germany's first woman rabbi, Regina Jonas, studied here from 1924–30. She was murdered in Auschwitz in 1944. Peak enrollment was in 1932, when 155 students attended.

With an outstanding faculty and a gifted student body, the College enjoyed an influence much greater than its numbers might indicate. Many of the most prominent and important Jewish thinkers of the time, including Leo Baeck, Martin Buber, and the philosopher Hermann Cohen, taught or lectured here. Other influential figures, such as Solomon Schechter, one of the founders of the Conservative movement in the United States (and the discoverer of the valuable early Jewish documents in the Genizah in Cairo), and the teacher and writer Abraham Joshua Heschel, were students. Attendees at its famous Monday night public lectures included Franz Kafka and Gershom Scholem. Although other buildings and landmarks, notably the New Synagogue, attract more attention than this rather dowdy structure, the College must be counted among the most important Jewish institutions in Berlin—if not in all of Europe—of the last century.

By the late 1930s, this was the sole rabbinical seminary open in Germany. The building was ransacked during the Kristallnacht pogrom on November 9–10, 1938, but allowed to remain open under Gestapo surveillance. On July 19, 1942, it was closed for good.

The simple plaque to the right of the entrance reads: "From the years 1907 to 1942, the College for the Science of Judaism, founded in 1872, was located in this house."

Double back to Oranienburger Strasse, turn right and continue to number 28, the Neue Synagoge *(New Synagogue).*

⓱ The New Synagogue has been a Berlin landmark since its construction in 1866. Distinctive and imposing, it was built as an emblem of the stature of the Berlin Jewish Community and was long an ornament for that Community, a nationally famous building in one of Europe's major cities. Its gilded onion dome, 160 feet above the street, quickly became a familiar part of the Berlin skyline.

The structure was designed by Eduard Knoblauch and completed after he fell ill by Friedrich Augustus Stüler. (Neither of the architects was Jewish.) Its "Moorish" architecture was popular at the time and considered especially appropriate where the prevailing style of religious buildings, Gothic revival, was to be avoided for its Christian connotations. The Dohany Utca synagogue in Budapest, completed in 1859, and Central Synagogue on Lexington Avenue in New York, from 1868, are other notable examples of this Moorish style.

The dedication, on September 5, 1866, was a major social event in Berlin. Among the many prominent figures who passed through the doors (under the Hebrew inscription from Isaiah 26:2, "Open the gates to let a righteous nation enter, a nation that keeps faith.") was Prussian Prime Minister Bismarck.

At the time this was Germany's largest synagogue. The main sanctuary seated 1800 in the men's section and 1200 in the women's gallery. Shabbat services, however, typically attracted only 300-400 worshippers, and the weekday services were held in a smaller room toward the front.

The importance of the New Synagogue within the community decreased somewhat over the years as other large synagogues were built and the fashionable areas shifted to the west of the city. However, it retained a cherished place in the hearts of Berlin's Jews and continued to serve as a city landmark.

On the night of November 9–10, 1938, as part of the Kristallnacht pogrom that destroyed synagogues and Jewish businesses across the country, SA men set fire to the New Synagogue's men's vestibule. Wilhelm Krützfeld, district police chief stationed down the street in Hackescher Markt, rushed over with a drawn pistol and a file with papers that declared that, because of its artistic and cultural value, the synagogue had been placed under police protection (a kind of early version of a landmark protection law). He and a couple of his men chased the SA cadre away and then ordered the fire department to put out the blaze. A plaque to commemorate his bravery has been placed outside the lobby entrance to the right of the synagogue. It reads: "During the pogrom night of November 9–10, 1938, the police official Wilhelm Krützfeld (1880–1953), with courageous and resolute intervention, preserved this synagogue from destruction. The Berlin Police Department."

It was one of the few synagogues allowed to open again after the pogrom, and weekly services were held, obviously under the most difficult of circumstances, until the week of April 12, 1940, when the Nazi government permanently put a halt to worship here. The Wehrmacht confiscated the building that same year, turning it into a warehouse for textiles and leather and outfitting some of the rooms as air-raid shelters. The structure was severely damaged during a British bombing raid on the night of November 22, 1943.

After the war, the small community of survivors and refugees reestablished itself here in undamaged rooms at Oranienburger Strasse 28, next door to the gutted and desecrated synagogue. There was neither the energy, nor the money, nor—for the small community that did not necessarily intend to stay—the need, to restore the synagogue. When the Jewish Community, along with the rest of the city, became divided, these conditions were intensified: the East German Jewish Community was miniscule, with only about 200 members, and the East German government, officially atheist and anti-Zionist, was not accomodating. In 1958, the ruins of the sanctuary were demolished, leaving only the front rooms and the facade of the structure.

The small East Berlin Jewish Community lobbied to have the facade preserved as a memorial. To mark the 100th anniversary of the synagogue, they affixed a tablet on the right side of the entrance. It reads: "This synagogue is 100 years old and was set on fire by the Nazis on Kristallnacht November 9, 1938. In 1943, during World War II 1939–45, it was destroyed by a bombing raid. The facade of this house of God should remain for all time as a place of admonition and remembrance. Never forget. The Executive Board of the Jewish Community of Greater Berlin. September 1966."

As a result of a change in East German government policy in the late 1980s toward Israel (and, some say, a pitch by East German head of state Erich Honecker to finagle a state visit to the US), it was decided to turn the building into a memorial and cultural center. In July 1988, the Centrum Judaicum–Neue Synagoge foundation was founded.

Four months later, on the anniversary of the Kristallnacht pogrom, a second tablet was installed, this one on the left side of the entrance, reading: "50 years after the desecration of this synagogue and 45 years after its destruction, this house will, by our will and with the support of many friends in our land and throughout the world, rise anew. Jüdische Gemeinde Berlin, 9 November 1988."

It was decided not to attempt a rebuilding of the synagogue, but rather to preserve the remnants as they were and to clearly indicate reconstruction and additions with modern designs. The only exceptions are the facade, where the new work is clearly marked with light yellow brick, and the onion domes that crown the building.

The Centrum Judaicum-Neue Synagoge Foundation enjoys a

high profile in the community. It organizes a wide range of stimulating exhibitions, maintains a permanent collection on the history of the synagogue and the surrounding neighborhood, sponsors readings and lectures, conducts research, and maintains an archive. The Foundation shares space in the building next door with the Jewish Community, which has a library and a social and educational center here. Included too in the complex is the Jüdische Galerie, an art gallery featuring artists from the former Soviet Union, and Cafe Oren, which specializes in Israeli food. In the rear courtyard, the Community has recently opened a new sports hall for the use of its students. The New Synagogue has again become a center of Jewish activity and a place of Jewish pride, as it was when built over a century ago.

Anti-Semitism Today

Anti-Semitic incidents in Berlin may echo louder and longer than those elsewhere, but the actual incidence of anti-Semitic acts in the city is relatively low.

According to official statistics, there were 112 anti-Semitic incidents in the city in 1995, 84 in 1996, and 96 in 1997. These mainly involved distribution of anti-Semitic material, instances of grafitti, and assaults on property—memorials and cemeteries for the most part.

There exists in some of the outlying districts of Berlin a distressingly lively neo-Nazi scene. This is less an organized political movement and more a youth subculture with its own style of dress (often shaved heads, bomber jackets, t-shirts and combat boots) and music. For all their lack of political sophistication, though, these young men are thuggish and dangerous. Fortunately these types rarely venture into central Berlin, and visitors to the city seldom have any reason to traipse out to suburbs such as Marzahn or Pankow.

Organized political parties with anti-Semitic tendencies have thus far been unable to attract durable support. The two largest are the Republikaners and the Deutsche Volksunion (German People's Union), each with, according to government figures, about 15,000 members nationwide and 700-800 members in Berlin.

Opinion polls indicate that anti-Semitic attitudes among the general population persist. A 1996 poll from Der Spiegel, the country's main weekly news magazine, showed that about 20% of Germans nationwide don't want a Jew as a neighbor and that almost one-third don't want to see a Jewish candidate for president. Other surveys have indicated that anti-Semitic opinions are more common among older people and among residents of the states of the former East Germany.

A disconcerting part of the Jewish Berlin experience for visitors is the frequent presence of police and security measures at Jewish sites. Police guards are posted at all Jewish insitutions, at synagogues when services are taking place, and often at other sites where Jews are gathering. Metal detectors are present at the Centrum Judaicum cultural center and sometimes at synagogues. These security measures can be irritating and distasteful; if it is any consolation, however, such security is present not only in Germany but throughout Europe.

12 | A History of Jewish Berlin

The Road to Equality: Origin to the end of World War I

Berlin's early years were humble, for its Jews as well as for its Gentiles. The Jewish community that developed here along with the small town enjoyed no repute. It could not boast of any renowned rabbis or scholars such as those long active further south in Worms, Speyer, and Mainz. It supported no accomplished scribes such as those in Heidelberg. Yet it eventually far surpassed these cities.

For a century and a half, from the late 1700s until the victory of Naziism, Berlin was home to the most dynamic Jewish community on the continent, a hotbed of religious modernization and innovation, and a beacon for Jewish talent.

Berlin was the home of the *Haskalah*, the Jewish Enlightenment; the nurturing ground for both the Reform and Conservative movements; and the birthplace of the academic discipline of Jewish Studies.

At the same time, the city was fertile ground for an explosion of secular talent in cultural and intellectual spheres, science and medicine, and business pursuits. The record of accomplishment of the Jews who flocked here from all over Europe is striking.

Origins and Exoduses

The first written record to mention the town of Berlin dates from 1244; the first written evidence of a Jewish presence in the town crops up just over 50 years later, in 1295: a letter from the Berlin city council forbidding merchants to supply Jews with wool yarn.

Most, but not all, of these Jews lived in the center of what was then a small village, segregated in the *Grosser Judenhof* (Great Jews' Court) and *Jüdenstrasse* (Jews' Street). The single trace remaining today of these medieval locations is *Jüdenstrasse*, which has survived in name for some seven hundred years (even during the years of the Third Reich) and still runs more or less along its original course.

Berlin's first Jews were involved mainly in trading, money

changing, and money lending. Life was difficult and well-taxed: Jews were dunned when marrying, circumsizing their sons, slaughtering in a kosher manner and burying their dead, to cite just a few examples.

Life was precarious as well, and a repeating cycle of persecution and expulsion dogged the Jews of Berlin. Blamed for the "Black Death" bubonic plague that ravaged the area in 1349–50, Jews were murdered or expelled. Survivors returned as early as 1354, and in 1446 their descendants were driven out again. In 1510, after being accused of desecrating a Host, and again in 1571, in the aftermath of the execution of the Court Jew and community leader Lippold, the Jewish residents of Berlin were murdered or banished.

The Modern Community

The beginning of the modern Jewish community in Berlin dates from 1671, when Emperor Frederick William of Prussia invited 50 well-off Jewish families recently expelled from Vienna to come to Berlin. The Prussian ruler's reasons were pragmatic rather than humanitarian: He was desperate to rebuild the economy and restock his treasury after the ruinous Thirty Years War (1618-1648) and looked to the Jews for capital, tax income, and entrepreneurial energy. At the same time and for the same reasons, Frederick William admitted Protestant Huguenots from France and other religious dissidents into the country.

The Edict of May 21, 1671 allowed these Jewish families to reside where they chose, engage in trade without restriction, and keep a slaughterer and a schoolteacher. It sounded magnanimous, and for the times, it was. However, there was a catch or two: the edict was to run for only twenty years, and each family was allowed to settle only one child in town. Additional children had to be sent away or hidden from the authorities. Ultimately, Berlin's Jewish community remained subject to the arbitary whims of the king, who was always on the lookout for revenue.

The privilege to build a public synagogue, for example, was granted in 1700 only after a payment of 3,000 Thalers to the crown. The new synagogue, in Heidereutergasse—widely admired for its elegance and gracefulness—was opened before the Jewish New Year in 1714 and was to serve as the city's sole public synagogue for the next 150 years.

Economic Activities

The major source of Jewish commercial activity in Berlin at the time was the royal court, and the main beneficiary the "court Jew," usually a combination moneylender, jeweler, and financial advisor. In Berlin, the most famous of these court Jews was Veitel Heine Ephraim, active around the middle of the eighteenth century. His mansion, the "Ephraim Palais," is still standing. Other prominent bankers and minters included Daniel Itzig and Moses and Elijah Gumperz. These wealthy figures formed the elite of the community and by virtue of their contacts with the court, they, rather than the rabbinate, served as leaders of the community.

Jews not attached to the court were relegated for the most part to modest occupations such as shopkeeping, pawnbroking and peddling. Over time, many Jews drifted into the city without permission. By 1750, among the two thousand Jews living in Berlin, some five hundred were there illegally, most of them very poor and all subject to expulsion at any time.

Slowly but surely the Jewish community drew nearer to the spiritual and cultural values of Prussian society. The Enlightenment ideals of tolerance and human dignity then emerging naturally attracted Jews. Championing this process of modernization was the great Enlightenment philosopher Moses Mendelssohn.

The German Socrates

Moses Mendelssohn, the "German Socrates," as he was known in his lifetime, rose from humble circumstances to prominence as the best-known and most influential Jew of his time, an honored philosopher and writer, and creator of the Jewish Enlightenment movement known, from the Hebrew, as *Haskalah*.

Mendelssohn was born in Dessau in 1729, the son of a poor Torah scribe, and came to Berlin as a young boy to further his education. Even in his teens he was voracious in his studies. Though his curved spine was due to a genetic disorder, Mendelssohn liked to say that it was caused by his early excessive study of Moses Maimonides: "Maimon gave me my hump, but I still dote on him for the many hours of dejection he converted into rapture. He weakened my body, but invigorated my soul."

It was by accident that Mendelssohn came upon a work of non-Hebrew philosophy. He was immediately captivated by the subject, by the Enlightment movement and by the world of ideas beyond the

Talmud. To gain entry into this world, he mastered in short order Latin, Greek, French, English, Italian, logic, geometry, and mathematics.

Thus armed, he went on to produce some of the major works of Enlightenment philosophy and earn an international reputation. In addition to the many general philosophical books and essays that he penned, several of his works defended Judaism and pleaded for equal rights. Others were written exclusively for his co-religionists. He produced a German translation of the Torah, works in Hebrew and, to introduce Jews to modern secular society, several works in German written in Hebrew characters. His writings fill seven volumes.

Religiously devout, Mendelssohn interpreted Judaism, in accordance with his Enlightenment beliefs, as a religion of reason, free of dogma. "The spirit of Judaism is conformity in action and freedom of theological opinion, except for a few fundamental doctrines of universal validity on which all our teachers agree and without which the Jewish religion itself could not exist."

In his writings and by personal example, Mendelssohn demonstrated that Jews, while remaining Jewish, could participate in and make important contributions to Western civilization. With Moses Mendelssohn, the emancipation—or better, the self-emancipation—of the Jews had begun.

The Heirs of Mendelssohn

When he died in 1786, the philosopher left behind a coterie of talented followers that spread *Haskalah* to Berlin and beyond. David Friedländer, acknowledged to be Mendelssohn's successor, founded a Free School for Jewish children in Berlin in 1778, the first school to combine secular subjects with traditional Jewish education. He was the first Jew appointed to the city council.

Other intellectuals in this circle included Daniel Itzig, co-founder of the Jewish Free School; philosopher Salomon Maimon; Abraham Euchels, who helped to found the first Hebrew-language magazine, *Ha-Meassef* (The Collector); and Marcus Herz, who studied with philosopher Immanuel Kant and later served as physician-in-chief of Berlin's Jewish Hospital.

These Jews, clean-shaven and bare-headed, were part of the first generation to reject the insular world of Talmud and Torah for the larger compass of western culture. Already in 1799, Friedländer wrote that "the ceremonial laws were observed in our fathers' houses with the most anxious punctiliousness. These estranged us from the sphere of ordinary life; as empty customs they produced no further effect on our behavior than to make us shy, embarrassed, and often uneasy ...."

The Jewish Salons

A first meeting point with German culture for many of the Jewish elite came in Berlin's salons. In the late eighteenth and early nineteenth century, dozens of these salons—gatherings of writers, artists, and thinkers in a private home—flourished, the best-known and most popular of them hosted by Jewish women. Most notable of these hostesses were Henriette Herz (wife of Marcus Herz), Dorothea Schlegel (daughter of Moses Mendelssohn), and Rahel Varnhagen. Their gatherings were considered the center of the intellectual and social life of Berlin.

Within the walls of their sitting rooms, people from all walks of life—and religions—could meet and talk, and regular visitors included the poet Heinrich Heine; playwright Heinrich von Kleist; the von Humboldt brothers, who founded Berlin's first university; Crown Prince Louis Ferdinand; and many other of the city's cultural stars. Though the salons were considered somewhat daring and their Jewish hostesses a touch exotic, the gatherings seemed to indicate a growing acceptance of Jews.

Integration and Excellence

Over the next several decades, acceptance, prominence even, was achieved by a handful of Jews (and Christians of Jewish origin) in the city. The most notable of these success stories was the composer Felix Mendelssohn, grandson of Moses. Felix Mendelssohn, baptized by his father at the age of 7, was a towering figure in the music world of his day, the initiator of the revival of the music of J.S. Bach, and world-famous for his *Scottish Symphony, Italian Symphony*, and music for *A Midsummer Night's Dream*, which includes his famous *Wedding March*.

As prominent was the Romantic writer Heinrich Heine, who spent a few years in Berlin, though much of the life of one of Germany's greatest poets was spent in exile in Paris. During his stay here he was a frequent visitor in the salon of Rahel Varnhagen, whom he called "the wittiest woman in the universe."

Opera composer Giacomo Meyerbeer, born Jacob Liebmann Beer, managed to achieve success without conversion. His grand historical operas such as *The Huguenots* made him one of the most popular composers of the day. From 1842 to 1847, he was royal director of the opera in Berlin, a rare state post for an unconverted Jew.

Journalist Ludwig Börne (like Heine, baptized), theater owner Karl Friedrich Cerf, journalist and politician Gabriel Riesser, and humorist David Kalisch were among others who made a name for themselves in that early Berlin cultural milieu. These artists and professionals struggled not only against popular anti-Semitism, but official barriers as well: non-Christians were ineligible for government posts, which included university professorships and civil service work, and most state-sponsored cultural positions.

First Stirrings of Emancipation

By the beginning of the nineteenth century, Berlin boasted 200,000 inhabitants and trailed only London and Paris in population. There were approximately 3,000 Jewish residents, still not citizens, still unequal before the law. For these Jews the first step toward legal emancipation came in 1806, when Napoleon's forces conquered Prussia and occupied Berlin. The revolutionary watchword "liberty, equality, fraternity" was naturally greeted with special enthusiasm by the Jewish community. Six years later, a French-installed reform government in Prussia turned that slogan into law—the Prussian Edict of 1812.

This law abolished all special taxes and payments and granted Jews full citizenship save for a restriction on state employment—meaning that, with few exceptions, Jews could not enter into military service, academic careers, or the civil service. Enfranchisement remained partial. Still, it was a significant step.

The Rise of German Nationalism

German liberals, Christians and Jews alike, initially welcomed the reforms set in motion by Napoleon. However, a reaction to French occupation soon set in and culminated in armed conflict and the defeat of Napoleon at Waterloo in 1815. Frederick William III was restored to the Prussian throne. As patriotic Prussians, many Jews fought to remove the French from their native soil.

The struggle for liberation from French occupation also involved a struggle against French Enlightenment notions and the championing of German chauvinism and nationalism. Along with such practical goals as self-rule and the unification of the many small German states, German nationalists embraced a romanticism that glorified a mythical, medieval German past and a timeless, ineffable German spirit. Jews shared neither this Christian past nor this Teutonic essence. They were thus considered by thoroughgoing nationalists as alien, indeed hostile, to the *Volk*,—the Germanic people—and thus not fit to enjoy the same social or legal status. As philosopher Johann Gottlieb Fichte bluntly put it: "the only way to give them citizenship would be to cut off all their heads on the same night in order to replace them with those containing no Jewish ideas."

The "Jewish Question," whether Jews could be part of the German polity without giving up the distinctiveness of their Judaism, was a hotly debated issue throughout the nineteenth century. The history of the Jews of Germany can be seen as an unceasing attempt—through conversion and reform, unstinting patriotism and loyalty, and secular achievement—to earn the right to be German, an attempt which, of course, ultimately failed.

Initially the only recourse for individual Jews was baptism, "the admission ticket to Western civilization," as Heine put it. Early nineteenth-century Berlin saw a wave of conversions of prominent Jews hoping to become fully accepted members of the Christian state. The fate of Moses Mendelssohn's children is a striking example of the pressures of the dominant culture. All but the eldest son of this pious Jew eventually converted to Protestantism.

Adaptations to Modernism

The overwhelming majority wished to retain their Judaism, and found other ways of responding to the pressures of modernity, emancipation, and nationalism. In 1819 three young men, Eduard Gans, Leopold Zunz, and Moses Moser, founded the *Verein für Cultur und Wissenschaft der Juden* (Society for Jewish Culture and Science) in Berlin. They wanted to develop a new approach to the study of Judaism, one that used modern academic methods of analysis and study and that was not limited to religious inquiry, but included philosophy, history, law, literature—the entire spectrum of human affairs.

In order to further their program, the Society organized lectures and meetings, published a "Periodical for the Science of Judaism" and established a library and archives. However, when two of the society's leading members, Eduard Gans, the president, and the poet Heinrich Heine, converted to Protestantism, the organization suffered a fatal blow and expired.

Despite the demise of the society, its aim of a dispassionate examination of Jewish history and customs remained to clear the way for reform of religious practices. Historical research indicated that many hoary Jewish traditions were really not so old, or were instituted in response to specific conditions that no longer existed. For instance, Leopold Zunz, who alone among the founders of the society remained dedicated to its goals, showed that sermons in the vernacular were once a regular part of the religious service, thereby refuting rabbis who had opposed the introduction of sermons in German as a modern innovation. Such scholarly detective work brought many practices into question and fueled a desire for reform.

First Stirrings of Reform

The first moves came from a wealthy businessman, Israel Jacobson, who in 1815 established a private synagogue in Berlin featuring a shortened liturgy in the German language accompanied by organ and choir. Jacobson's innovations proved immediately popular, but also aroused fierce opposition from Orthodox elements of the community, who appealed to the conservative Prussian government for a ban. The government obliged in 1823.

Still, the endeavor to define Judaism—as Moses Mendelssohn did—as a religion of reason with universal ideas could not be stopped. In 1845, another reform congregation was founded in Berlin. Guiding it was the rather radical Samuel Holdheim, a former Orthodox rabbi. Denying the authority of the *Halacha* as binding legislation, Holdheim tried to adapt the contemporary practice of Jewish ritual to the Christian environment. He shifted the Sabbath celebrations to Sunday, abolished the observance of the second day of holidays, eliminated the wearing of tallis and skull cap, and introduced mixed seating during services.

Holdheim's ideas were too radical for most Jews, and his congregation always remained at the extreme margin of the Berlin community. But, carried over the seas by Jewish emigrants, his notions had a significant influence on the course of the Reform movement in the United States.

More popular was a moderate adaptation of Judaism to modern

German life. In religious services, sermons in German and choirs became increasingly popular and attempts were made to instill decorum in the synagogue.

The Orthodox Response

By the second half of the century, the increasing liberalization of the official, state-sanctioned Jewish Community organization had created a backlash. In 1869, Orthodox members pulled out to form their own independent congregation, Adass Yisroel, headed by the dynamic Esriel Hildesheimer. Together with Samuel Raphael Hirsch in Frankfurt, Hildesheimer was a leader of the German neo-Orthodox movement, which renounced any deviation whatsoever from *Halacha*. He did not, however, reject secular learning nor Jewish historical studies as long as they served to bolster Torah and Talmud, and in 1873 he established in Berlin the country's leading orthodox rabbinical seminary.

The New Synagogue

Although tension between the Orthodox and Liberal wings of the community had been brewing for years, the immediate cause for the split was the introduction of an organ and choir when the New Synagogue was opened in 1866.

This house of worship, the city's first major new synagogue since the Heidereutergasse shul built 150 years before, was a statement of the self-confidence and pride of Berlin's Jewish community, which had in the meantime grown to become the largest and most important in Germany. The imposing Moorish building—with seating for 3,000 it was the largest synagogue in the country— was set proudly on the street line, in contrast to the usual German habit of tucking synagogues in back courtyards. When Prussian Prime Minister Otto von Bismarck himself attended the opening, Berlin's Jews felt they had surely arrived.

Emancipation and Success

By most measures, they had. By the middle of the nineteenth century, Germany's startlingly rapid industrial growth had created the world's third largest economy. Economic expansion was bolstered by German unification in 1871, when most of the small German states were united under the leadership of Prussia, and Berlin became the capital of this second German Reich (the first was the

Holy Roman Empire, which flourished in the Middle Ages). Many Jews shared in this prosperity, and economic success and social integration reinforced their identification with German society and German culture.

It was at this time that Jews finally won formal emancipation and the last legal barriers to unhindered participation in German society fell. De facto strictures remained, however, particularly in the military, the judiciary, academia, and the higher levels of the civil service.

In compensation, emergent capitalism opened up new sectors to Jews—manufacturing, retailing and professions such as medicine, law, and journalism. Berlin became one of Europe's major metropoles, a dynamic, cosmopolitian and liberal city that attracted Jews from all over Germany and Eastern Europe. The Jewish population of the capital city jumped from 12,675 in 1855 (2.9% of the total population) to 36,326 in 1871 (4.1%), as Jews left the small towns of the countryside—where they were traditionally restricted to petty trading and cattle dealing—for the opportunities of the city.

Success Stories

Jewish prominence in the field of banking—a tradition stretching back to the court Jews of pre-Enlightenment days—continued in late nineteenth-century Berlin. There were more than 30 private Jewish banks (out of a total of 52), many of them long-established family businesses such as Mendelssohn & Co., founded by two of the sons of Moses Mendelssohn.

Another Berlin Jewish banker, Gerson Bleichröder, was the financial advisor to Chancellor Bismark and the German government for more than three decades. He was the first German Jew to be ennobled without undergoing baptism.

The department store, an idea imported from the United States, was a modern institution in which Berlin Jews were extremely successful. This new style of shopping, with fixed, low prices, a wide variety of items, and returnable goods, all in elegant surroundings, revolutionized consumers' habits. A pioneer of the department store was Nathan Israel, who developed a small fabric shop, opened in 1815, into one of the city's most popular large stores. Similar literal rags-to-riches stories were experienced by other successful department store entrepreneurs such as Hermann Tietz, Hermann Gerson, Arthur Wertheim, and Adolf Jandorf, the founder of Kaufhaus des Westens (KaDeWe).

The transformation of newspapers into mass market publications was forged by Jewish publishers such as Rudolf Mosse and Leopold Ullstein. Mosse, who founded the *Berliner Tageblatt* in 1874, was the first to use advertising as a principal source of newspaper revenue. Ullstein bought the *Berliner Zeitung* in 1877 and eventually built an empire consisting of newspapers, books and magazines. The Berlin bookseller Samuel Fischer founded a publishing company in 1886 that became one of Germany's leading literary publishers.

The second half of the nineteenth century also saw the first significant participation by Jews in electoral politics. Jewish politicians ranged over the entire political spectrum, from the arch-conservatism of Friedrich Julius Stahl (a convert to Protestantism) to the radicalism of Ferdinand Lassalle, founder of the General Association of German Workers. Berlin Jewish voters, however, were overwhelmingly attracted to moderate middle-class parties such as the National Liberal Party, led by Eduard Lasker and Ludwig Bamberger. In the 1860s and '70s, the National Liberal Party attracted around 70% of the Jewish vote.

Religious Developments

Worldly success was often accompanied by a loss of religious faith. The erosion of religious observance proceeded earlier and more thoroughly in Germany than just about anywhere else: it was here that the "twice-a-year Jew" first emerged.

But the situation was far from one-sided, for at the same time there was great vitality in some areas of religious affairs. Inspired by the ideas of Leopold Zunz's "Science of Judaism," Abraham Geiger and several other scholars established a liberal rabbinical seminary called the *Hochschule für die Wissenschaft des Judentums* (College for the Science of Judaism) in 1872. Geiger, the first director of the college, was one of the main theoreticians of reform and an untiring proponent of a Jewish faith compatible with modern ideas and lifestyles.

The seminary, dedicated to pure scholarship as well as training rabbis, had a huge influence on the Conservative and Reform movements. Many of the most important Jewish thinkers of the time, including Leo Baeck and Martin Buber, taught there. Other influential figures, such as Solomon Schechter, one of the founders of the Conservative movement in the United States, and the teacher and writer Abraham Joshua Heschel, were students.

The very next year, the Orthodox Adass Yisroel congregation founded its own seminary, the *Rabbinerseminar zu Berlin* (The Rabbinical Seminary of Berlin). The first Orthodox seminary in Germany, it also showed the stamp of German culture: it included in its curriculum not only secular subjects, but also a requirement that students simultaneously complete a degree at the University of Berlin. Thus the city was home to two of the country's three rabbinical seminaries.

Immigration from the East

Beginning in the 1880s, the Jewish milieu was enlivened as well by a wave of *Ostjuden* (eastern European Jews), fleeing misery in Austria-Hungary or pogroms in Russia and part of the same exodus that brought so many Jews to North America and Great Britain. These Jews from eastern Europe were a world apart from the bourgeois Berlin Jews: They generally spoke Yiddish, wore traditional shtetl garb, and took their Judaism seriously. Most of them were working-class or petty traders and poor. By the 1920s, these immigrants made up one-fifth of the Jewish population of Germany.

The encounter of bourgeois German Jew and eastern shetl Jew was not necessarily a warm one. The immigrants were a cause of consternation and embarrassment for the staid German Jews. Having invested a century in assimiliation, they viewed the *Ostjuden*—the term itself was pejorative—with distaste.

Outburst of Anti-Semitism

German Jews in Berlin felt, by and large, well-off and content during the Second Reich (1871–1918). They could be gratified by the attainment of legal emancipation. They could point with satisfaction to the contributions—economic and cultural—made to their society. Most of all, they could take great pride in their homeland, a powerful, united and enlightened country of the first rank. German Jews were passionately—chauvinistically—German. Their exclusion from certain social clubs, or fraternities, or professions, they had come to regard as an old-fashioned vexation soon to disappear.

It came as a great shock to these Jews, then, when a powerful anti-Semitic political movement suddenly erupted in the last decades of the century. In 1879, Wilhelm Marr, a journalist, published a pamphlet entitled "The Victory of Judaism over Germanism." It revived "the Jewish Question" as a public topic once again and sparked an outpouring of anti-Jewish political activity known as the "Berlin Movement."

That same year Marr founded the Anti-Semitic League, thereby popularizing the word that was to loom so large in German history. Politician and clergyman Adolf Stöcker, who served as the court preacher for the royal family, turned his Christian Social Workers Party into a powerful political force by adopting the League's anti-Jewish rhetoric. The entire movement was given respectability by the renowned historian Heinrich von Treitschke, who coined the notorious slogan later adopted by the Nazis: "The Jews are our misfortune."

An anti-Semitic petition calling the curtailment of Jewish rights was circulated around the country, amassing 225,000 signatures. On New Years' Eve, 1880, organized gangs rampaged down Unter den Linden, shouting *Juden raus!* (Jews get out!) and assaulting Jewish patrons in cafés.

In 1890, five candidates running on an anti-Semitic platform were elected to the Reichstag; in 1893, there were 16; elections the next year resulted in 24. But the movement had actually lost momentum by the mid-1880s; Marr and Stöcker and their parties failed to attract a permanent base and faded. The 1894 election was the high point in anti-Semitic electoral strength, and even by then the subject had faded as a public issue.

Among the causes of this first outbreak of modern anti-Semitism were the dislocations of rapid industrialization, growing nationalism, a depression beginning in 1873, the immigration of Jews from the east, and the visible success of Jews in the capitalist economy.

Fighting Back

The strength of the Berlin Movement revealed to Jews that their position was more precarious than they had thought. To defend their rights and reputations, the *Centralverein deutscher Staatsbürger jüdischen Glaubens* (Central Association of German Citizens of Jewish Faith) was founded in Berlin in 1893. The *Centralverein* served as a self-defense organization to combat anti-Semitism through legal action, through educational campaigns, and through opposition to anti-Semitic political candidates. The

Centralverein grew to become the largest and most important national Jewish organization. It was also one of the few that united most of the religious strains of German Jewry: in Berlin, even the independent Orthodox Adass Yisroel congregation, which usually rejected alliances with reform groups, was affiliated.

The formation of the *Centralverein* was a decisive and somewhat painful step: German Jews, who for so long had tried to meld into German culture, now had to assert themselves as Jews. The *Centralverein* called for the "right to call ourselves Germans, without baptism and so-called assimilation," as Eugen Fuchs, later president of the organization, wrote in 1912.

A different route to self-defense was taken by a new Jewish movement lately sprung from the pen of the Austrian journalist Theodor Herzl: Zionism. Just four years after the founding of the *Centralverein*, the *Zionistische Vereinigung für Deutschland* (the German Zionist Federation) was organized. Berlin served not only as the seat of the national organization, but was also headquarters of the World Zionist Organization from 1911–20.

Although insisting, in contrast to the large majority of German Jews, that Jews comprised a nationality and that Palestine was the Jewish homeland, the early German Zionists were quite moderate. They were careful not to alienate their prosperous and patriotic fellow German Jews and presented Zionism mainly as a vehicle for promoting Jewish self-consciousness and pride. Emigration was not stressed, and Palestine was depicted as a homeland for the huddled masses of eastern European Jewry, not for their fellow countrymen. Despite such soft-pedaling, the Zionists remained a modest movement in Germany. By 1914 the movement had less than 10,000 members nationwide, and probably no more than 2,000 German Jews ever made *aliyah* before the assumption of power by the Nazis.

A Call to Arms

When world war broke out among the European powers on August 4, 1914, even the Zionists joined in the patriotic war hysteria. "German Jews!" the Zionist newspaper cried out, "We call on you . . .with all your heart, with all your soul and with all your means, to pledge your service to the Fatherland."

Emperor Wilhelm II's ringing call to arms, *"Ich kenne keine Parteien mehr und auch keine Konfessionen mehr; wir sind heute alle deutsche Brüder und nur noch deutsche Brüder!"*—I no longer recognize parties or creeds, today we are all German brothers and nothing but German brothers!—sounded to Jews like the long-awaited affirmation of their place in the German bosom.

Jews—secular and Orthodox, proletarian and bourgeois, assimilationist and Zionist—marched proudly to war with their Gentile countrymen. Some 100,000 German Jews took part in the conflict; about 12,000 perished.

The Illusion of Integration: The Weimar Republic

Germany was unmade by its defeat in the First World War. After four years of bloody stalemate and then capitulation, the country—war-weary, economically ruined, incompetently led—fell apart. Rioting that began among mutinous sailors in the northern port of Kiel in late October 1918, flared into civil war in Berlin, where fighting raged in the streets among communists, socialists, rightists and monarchists. On November 9, Kaiser Wilhelm II abdicated. A parliamentary republic was declared by moderate Social Democratic Party leaders and, almost simultaneously, a Russian-style Soviet system of workers' councils was announced by the radical left-wing Spartacist movement.

The communist bid for power was eventually crushed by the parliamentarians, though they had to move their assembly to the town of Weimar to escape the violence. Among the casualties of the fighting was the dynamic communist leader Rosa Luxemburg, a Jew from Poland, who was murdered on January 15, 1919 by nationalists. She has since become a left-wing hero, and a memorial now stands where her body was dumped in Tiergarten park.

Slowly, calm returned. The government moved back to Berlin and began the process of establishing democratic structures in a country accustomed to authoritarianism. But stability and legitimacy were elusive. The Weimar Republic's birth in the humiliation of defeat made it unpopular. A profusion of small parties made governing difficult. Economic problems, such as the hyperinflation of 1923–24, when a loaf of bread cost millions of marks, exacerbated the situation. Somehow, the spirit of democracy never took root.

Jews in Power
Several Berlin Jews were in top positions in the early Weimar

Republic government. Hugo Haase and Otto Landsberg were members of the provisional government after the Kaiser's flight to Holland; Hugo Preuss prepared the constitution; Walther Rathenau, son of the founder of Germany's General Electric Company, was an early foreign minister. In the city, too, Jews found opportunities for public service in the local district councils and city administration, most prominently Fritz Elsas, who was the mayor of Berlin from 1931–33.

On the one hand, this participation augured well for Jews in the new republic. On the other hand, it did not escape the attention or agitation of their enemies. Germany's fragile new democracy was dubbed "The Jew Republic" by anti-Semites, who also charged that the Weimar politicians had stabbed Germany in the back by signing the hated Treaty of Versailles, which demanded onerous reparations and an admission of German responsibility for the war.

Walter Rathenau was the first victim of this calumny. A deeply patriotic man, he had worked tirelessly as chief of the War Materials Office before his appointment as foreign minister in 1922. "I have no other blood than German, no other people than German," he wrote in 1916. Neither his service to the state nor his chauvinism proved sufficient. On June 24, 1922, he was assassinated near his home in the Grunewald district of Berlin by right-wing nationalists.

Thunder on the Right
Political instability fed the growth of many small far-right parties. Decommissioned soldiers organized themselves into small paramilitary groups, called *Freikorps*, which battled communists in the streets and ocassionally threatened to bring down the government. Small splinter groups abounded; one of these, the *Deutsch-Völkisch Schutz- und Trutz Bund* (The German National League for Defense and Defiance), founded in 1919, adopted an old symbol for their ultranationalist and anti-Semitic ideology: the swastika.

These developments can now be seen as ominous harbingers, but at the time these hatemongers appeared harmless and irrelevant. Until the late 1920s, anti-Semitic parties never achieved much political success. In the Reichstag elections of December 7, 1924, for example, the entire vote for explicitly anti-Semitic parties was less than five percent of the total, and Jews, reasonably, felt unthreatened.

Weimar Culture Explodes

Rather, the Jewish community shared the excitement of most Berliners at the rising stature of their city as a European cultural capital and a center of artistic experimentation. There is much myth in the decadent and thrilling Berlin of "Cabaret," but some truth to it as well. A spirited, youthful liveliness embraced the once staid Prussian city, fueling a frenetic nightlife in over 70 cafés and cabarets, sparking artistic experiments such as Dada and expressionism and the modernist architecture of the Bauhaus school. Berlin, embracing the bold and novel and daring, overtook Paris as Europe's cultural magnet.

Jews participated fully in the new vistas that opened up in theater, film, music, journalism, and other urban arts, which also served as important means of Jewish cultural integration.

The Jewish Touch

Esssential contributions to the exceptional energy and vitality of German theater at this time, for example, were made by Jews such as theater director and producer Max Reinhardt and his rival Leopold Jessner, actors Alexander Granach and Elisabeth Bergner, and theater critics such as Alfred Kerr, Siegfried Jacobson and Julius Bab, to name only a few.

The most successful theater production of the time, Bertolt Brecht and Kurt Weill's musical *Die Dreigroschenoper* (The Threepenny Opera) seemed also to define the age with its wry irony and bitter wit. Weill, the son of a cantor, was responsible for the music, including the still popular "Mackie Messer" (Mac the Knife).

Another successful songwriter was Friedrich Holländer, many of whose songs were sung by Marlene Dietrich. The biggest stars of all in the popular music field were the Comedian Harmonists, a Berlin-based singing group, whose smooth harmonies made them nationwide sensations. Three of the six members, including founder Harry Frommermann, were Jewish.

Well-known but outside the realm of popular music were composers Arnold Schoenberg, developer of the twelve-tone scale, Hans Eisler and Paul Dessau, and conductors such as Otto Klemperer and Leo Blech.

In the newest artistic medium of the time, film, Jewish directors such as Ernst Lubitsch, Carl Mayer, and G.W. Pabst played prominent roles. Without Erich Pommer, the highly gifted producer and patron, the golden age of German film in the Weimar Republic would be unthinkable.

The mass circulation Ullstein and Mosse newspapers featured well-known Jewish editors and writers such as Theodor Wolff and Egon Erwin Kisch. (It should be mentioned, though, that despite the notable Jewish presence in much of the press of the day, the largest circulation newspaper belonged to Alfred Hugenberg, head of the anti-Semitic German Nationalist People's Party.)

Several Berlin-based Jewish novelists, poets and essayists attained recognition in the inter-war years. Among them were Alfred Döblin, who portrayed the pulsating city life of the capital in his famous novel *Berlin Alexanderplatz*, and Kurt Tucholsky, whose satires and essays attacked the hypocrisy of Weimar politics and society. Arnold Zweig expressed the tragedy of the First World War in his brilliant novel *The Case of Sergeant Grischa*, and Else Lasker-Schüler, one of the most gifted poets of her generation, attained prominence with her expressionistic love poems.

In scientific fields there were many Jews of note. Most eminent of them, of course, was Albert Einstein. He came to Berlin in 1913, already famous in scientific circles, to direct the Kaiser Wilhelm Institute of Physics, and received the Nobel Prize in physics in 1921. But Einstein was not the only Nobel Prize winner of Jewish descent active in the German capital. Max Born, who worked in the field of electronics, chemists Fritz Haber (baptized) and Richard Willstätter, and the physiologist Otto Meyerhof also deserve mention.

This laundry list of names (and it could be much longer) hints at the startling level of achievement of Berlin Jews in Weimar culture. While Jews participated actively in the intellectual and artistic life of the Weimar period, it should be kept in mind that they did so, in the overwhelming majority of cases, as assimilated Jews making secular contributions to secular culture. There was nothing specifically or intrinsically Jewish in their work.

Reassertion of Religion

Yet the energy of secular Weimar culture had its counterpart in the religious sphere. The post-First World War years witnessed a new dynamism in Jewish thinking, an affirmation of the value of the ancient religion in the modern world. There was a new willingness to highlight the differences between Judaism and Christianity, rather than, as in much of the nineteenth century, an inclination to stress the similarities.

Leo Baeck was the outstanding representative in Berlin of this movement. Baeck served as a rabbi in the large synagogue in Fasanenstrasse, directed the College for the Science of Judaism, and was the author of many religious and philosophical works including the bestselling (and still in print) *Das Wesen des Judentums (The Essence of Judaism)*. Immensely popular, he was acknowledged in his time as the outstanding leader of German Judaism. Defining Judaism as a nonconformist religion, he strongly resisted any interpretation of the basic doctrines of Judaism as dogmas. Baeck stressed the idea that each generation had to find its own religious expression and search for its own religious identity, rather than accept faith in fixed formulas.

Philosopher Martin Buber was another outspoken proponent of a vital Judaism. Buber tried to reach a synthesis of rabbinical Judaism and Chasidism, mediating between traditional Jewishness and new philosophical approaches to Jewish ideas. In the center of Buber's philosophy, expressed in his famous book *I and Thou*, published in 1923, stood the idea of dialog, the relationship between humans and God, humans and the world, humans and fellow humans.

A Magnet for Hebrew

There were other signs of renewal. In the 1920s, Berlin was a leading center of the modern Hebrew-language revival. Among the several Hebrew writers who lived and worked here were, most notably, the poet Chaim Nachman Bialik and the writer S.Y. Agnon, winner of the Nobel Prize in 1966.

Jewish and Hebrew publishers—among them Bialik's Dvir Publishing House (still a leading literary publisher in Israel), and the *Jüdischer Verlag* (Jewish Publishing House) founded in 1902 by a group of young Zionists, including Buber and Chaim Weizmann, later to become Israel's first president—issued a number of significant works in Hebrew, including the first collection by cultural Zionist Achad Ha'am. Simon Dubnow, the famous historian, produced his monumental *World History of the Jewish People* and a fully illustrated Jewish encyclopaedia, the *Jüdisches Lexikon*, was completed.

Zionism played a large role in this renewal, though it continued to be very much a minority movement. As late as 1929, the Zionist

Federation still boasted only about 20,000 members in Germany, 3.5% of the Jewish population of the country. Still, they displayed an energy and zeal outweighing their numbers.

Yet, continuing the trend of the nineteenth century, the larger Jewish community was overwhelmingly nonobservant and increasingly indifferent. In the 1920s, membership in the Community, bolstered by the continuing arrivals from the east, reached 172,000 (4.3% of the city's population), but few were observant. The large new synagogues of the city built during the second decade of the century— on Levetzowstrasse, Fasanenstrasse and Frankelufer (of all three, only a wing of the latter survives)—were close to empty for weekday services. Even for the High Holy Days, only about half of the Community membership during the late '20s bothered to attend synagogue.

The Rise of the Nazis

The Weimar Republic, after enjoying some stability in the mid-'20s, began to deteriorate under the effects of the Great Depression, which put one out of four Berliners out of work; a leadership uncommitted to democracy; and an inability to form majority coalitions in the Reichstag. The middle-class liberal parties in the center of the political spectrum that were favored by Jewish voters were increasingly viewed as enervated and lost votes to the socialist Social Democratic Party, the Communist Party of Germany, and the recently formed but quickly growing National Socialist German Workers' Party—the Nazis.

The Nazi Party was founded in January 1919 in Munich by railroad worker Anton Drexler and journalist Karl Harrer. Adolf Hitler joined the miniscule group—there were only about 50 card-carrying members—in September of that year and quickly rose to the leadership position. In the chaos following Germany's defeat in the First World War, there were dozens of similar ultra-nationalist, anti-Semitic parties. The Nazis distinguished themselves by their rejection of the traditional conservative pillars of monarchy, army, and landed gentry; their appeal to the middle class; and, especially, the tireless and charismatic leadership of Hitler.

Though the Nazis attracted attention with their aggressive tactics and streetfighting, they were not considered a serious political force until the elections of September, 1930, when they shot to prominence by garnering 18.3% of the votes nationwide (14.6% in

Berlin). This hoisted them from the ninth and smallest party in the parliament to the number two position. By the elections of July 1932, the Nazis—vociferously anti-democratic, aggressively chauvinistic, violent, and Jew-hating—had become the country's favorite party, polling 13,745,000 votes (37%) nationwide.

In Berlin, long considered a radical stronghold, the Nazis, drawing 28.7% of the vote, for the first time pulled ahead of the Social Democratic Party and the Communist Party. When the vote of the far-right German National People's Party is added to the Nazi total, it can be seen that, even in the supposedly cosmopolitan capital of Germany, some 37% of the electorate voted for explicitly anti-Semitic parties.

Fighting against the Nazi Tide

While most Jews, like many Gentiles, considered the Nazis a passing aberration, they did not stand idly by. Officials of the Jewish Community repeatedly petitioned the government to reign in the Nazis and particularly the SA, their paramilitary wing. They sponsored educational initiatives to counter Nazi slander and promote tolerance. Lawyers such as Hans Litten and Alfred Apfel took Nazis to court in several notorious cases, such as the trial resulting from the organized Nazi assaults against Jewish passersby on Kurfürstendamm on Rosh Hashanah in 1931.

The *Centralverein*, which had been fighting anti-Semitism since 1893, maintained a close watch on the militant organization, and kept up its tactics of bringing actionable cases to court, publicly refuting anti-Semitic defamation in its newspapers and brochures, and funding democratic parties. In addition, in 1929 they opened a separate office to deal exclusively with the National Socialist Party.

Other groups prepared for more aggressive action. The *Reichsbund jüdischer Frontsoldaten* (National League of Jewish Frontline Soldiers), a patriotic veterans' organization established to fight against the depressingly widespread notion that Jews had not contributed fully to the German war effort in the First World War, assembled secret arms caches in some cities, including Berlin, to defend themselves in case of pogroms. In 1927, following organized Nazi assaults on Jews in Berlin, they joined with several other Jewish groups to form an armed Jewish Defense Service. Jews also participated in other anti-fascist self-defense groups such as the *Reichsbanner*, a paramilitary group affiliated with the Social

Democratic Party.

All, obviously, to little avail. Jewish efforts—for the most part appeals to reason and the rule of law—were no match for the poisonous tide of Nazism. On January 30, 1933, Adolf Hitler was appointed chancellor of Germany.

Flight & Destruction: The Third Reich

With Hitler's appointment as chancellor and the Nazi success in the elections he called on March 5, 1933 (the Nazis received 43.9% of the national vote; 34.6% of the vote in Berlin) it was understood, even at the time, that the Weimar Republic had come to an end and a new chapter in German history opened. A huge wave of impassioned patriotism bouyed the Nazis and their "national revolution," and the eradication over the next few months of civil liberties, freedom of the press, opposition parties, and representative democracy was accomplished not just with a surprising lack of resistance but with a great deal of support. With little dissension and with a semblance of legality, the Nazi movement had within a few months turned Germany into a totalitarian state in which anti-Semitism was a core value.

The flight of Germany's artists and intelligentsia, those who had made Berlin a center of European culture, began almost immediately. "An exodus such as the world had never before seen," declared Bertolt Brecht, himself a part of this emigration. Jews, so prominent in the capital's culture, were also prominent among its exiles: novelist Alfred Döblin; poet Nelly Sachs, a Nobel Prize winner; Vicki Baum, author of *Grand Hotel*; Lion Feuchtwanger, author of *Jew Suss*; critics Walter Benjamin and Alfred Kerr; theater director Max Reinhardt; film director Billy Wilder; scientists Albert Einstein and fellow Nobel Prize winner Fritz Haber; and many, many others.

Anti-Semitism as official policy

Harrassment and raids by the police and the SA directed against the Eastern European *Ostjuden* in the Scheunenviertel began as early as March 1933, but the first concerted effort by the Nazi government directed against the Jews was the nationwide boycott of Jewish businesses on April 1, 1933. Posters, especially evident in the shopping districts around Leipziger Strasse in the center of town and Wittenbergplatz, Tauentzienstrasse and Kurfürstendamm in the west, were plastered on store windows: "Germans! Defend yourselves! Don't buy from Jews!" SA men stood by to hinder entrance. The offices of Jewish lawyers and doctors received the same treatment and were subject to stickers that read: "Attention Jew! Visit forbidden!" The boycott was originally planned to last longer, but fear of economic disruption and the generally tepid public response kept it to just one day.

Another portentous action took place on the night of May 19, 1933, when thousands of Berlin University students marched down Unter den Linden to Opernplatz (today Bebelplatz) opposite the university and, in a huge bonfire, burned some 25,000 books. Among the works destroyed—"perverters of the pure German spirit," according to the arsonist students—were those of Jewish authors such as Moses Mendelssohn, Henrich Heine, Albert Einstein, Franz Kafka, and Walter Rathenau.

These two incidents made clear that the Nazi movement had no intention of moderating its aim, stated clearly in the party's platform of 1920, to "combat the Jewish-materialist spirit within and without us" and to remove German Jews from the economy, culture, and society. Hopes that the chancellorship would moderate Hitler's anti-Semitism proved unfounded.

Lawful and Popular Persecution

On April 7, 1933, "The Law for the Restoration of the Professional Civil Service," was promulgated. This forbid those of "non-Aryan descent" to hold positions in the civil service. (The term "Aryan," as used by the Nazis, designated a fictitious race of all Northern Europeans who were not Jewish.)

■ **Steps to Destruction**

1933

■ **March 30:**
The state-run health insurance agency denies payment of claims to Jewish doctors, dentists, opticians, pharmacies and clinics.

■ **March 31:**
Jewish judges are forced to "retire."

■ **Beginning of April:**
Jewish teachers at state schools are forced to "retire."

■ **April 1:**
Boycott of Jewish-owned businesses.

■ **April 7:**
"Law for the Restoration of the Professional Civil Service" expels Jews from the civil service.

■ **April 25:**
Quotas introduced limiting Jewish enrollment in schools and universities to the percentage of Jews in the general population.

■ **Beginning of May:**
Jews denied entry to public sports fields, gymnasiums, and youth centers.

■ **August 22:**
Jews are no longer allowed to swim at the Wannsee Lake public beach.

Jewish civil servants (excluding some First World War veterans), were summarily fired. Over the next three years, subsequent decrees legally expelled a large number of Jews—doctors, jurists, professors and schoolteachers, actors, singers, journalists, and others—from their professions.

The Nuremberg Laws of September 15, 1935, were the capstone of this first phase of Nazi persecution. The "Law for the Protection of German Blood and German Honor" forbade marriages and sexual relations between Jews and Gentiles. The "Reich Citizenship Law," more importantly, officially made Jews non-citizens. With this law, the emancipation of the Jews, achieved through two hundred years of struggle and thought to have been permanently established half a century before, was obliterated.

These state measures were accompanied by a wave of popular anti-Semitism that resulted, without government compulsion, in the expulsion of Jews from private sector businesses and countless voluntary groups and professional organizations, from the National Chess Association to the German Association of Pharmacists; in the harrassment of Jews by students and teachers in schools and universities; and in the exclusion of Jews from a wide range of public facilities such as theaters, restaurants, hotels and the like.

Jewish Reactions

Jews reacted to the Nazi assumption of power and to the Nazification of German society with disbelief and dismay. Journalist Peter Wyden, a young teenager at the time, recalled, "In my family and among my friends, Hitler was tolerated with bemusement. We thought of him as a nut who had, by some inadvertence, been temporarily permitted to ascend to a position of power." The prominent painter Max Liebermann was more biting. Gazing from his window at a torchlight victory parade of the SA along Unter den Linden, he remarked, "One can't eat as much as one would like to vomit."

Jewish institutions, for the most part, urged a cautious "wait and see" attitude, but proceeded to meet the challenges that were swiftly presented to them. Representatives of community boards and major organizations came together in September 1933, to create the *Reichsvertretung der deutschen Juden* (National Representation of German Jews). This body, the first viable nationwide German Jewish organization to bring together all currents of German Judaism, from Orthodox to Zionist, attempted to find and coordinate responses to Nazi persecution, administrate welfare support for the increasing number of impoverished Jews, foster cultural and educational activities to sustain the community, and abet emigration from Germany.

The venerated Leo Baeck, the most famous German rabbi of his time, headed up the new organization. At its first meeting, he presciently declared: "The thousand-year history of German Jewry is at an end"—a warning regarded by just about everyone else as overly pessimistic. Operating under extreme conditions, the achievements of the *Reichsvertretung* were nonetheless notable.

Together with other Jewish organizations such as the *Zentralwohlfahrtstelle* (Central Welfare Agency) and the Berlin Jewish Community, the *Reichsvertretung* supported various schemes to aid the burgeoning number of unemployed Jews: already by June, 1933, more than a third of Berlin's Jewish white-collar employees, and almost half of the blue-collar workers, were jobless. The most notable of these initiatives was the *Jüdische Winterhilfe* (Jewish Winter Aid), a collection drive to provide foodstuffs and other direct support to the needy. The *Winterhilfe* stemmed from a similar drive set up in the last years of the Weimar Republic, a program that also served as the inspiration for a separate Nazi-sponsored *Winterhilfe* that excluded Jews. In 1935, Jewish Winter Aid was supporting nearly 30,000 Jewish Berliners, almost 20% of the entire Jewish population.

Getting Out

Most Jewish institutions, including the Berlin Jewish Community and the *Reichsvertretung*,

December:
Jews are expelled from all Berlin sports clubs.

1934

March 5:
Jewish actors are forbidden to work in their profession.

September 20:
Jewish youth groups are forbidden to wear uniforms or carry banners, to parade together, to hike together, or to spend the night in a tent or room together.

1935

March 31:
Jewish musicians are forbidden to work in their profession.

July 16:
Jews denied entry to all public pools and baths.

July 25:
Jews excluded from active military service.

September 15:
The Nuremberg Laws, the "Reich Citizenship Law" and the "Law for the Protection of German Blood and German Honor" disenfranchise Jews and forbid marriages and sexual relations between Jews and Gentiles.

October 4:
The police are empowered, on a case by case basis, to prohibit the construction of sukkahs.

recognized early the need to encourage emigration, even if only as an interim measure until sense and the rule of law returned to Germany. It was, nevertheless, a bold decision considering the deep feelings that most German Jews had for their homeland. The Community devoted much energy to advising members about emigration, steering them through the maze of applications, visa requirements, costs, likely destinations, transportation, and the like. The *Reichsvertretung* funded vocational training to provide skills for those seeking to leave, and organized a program to place children in special schools in England and Scotland.

The Zionist movement, which had of course long been promoting emigration, expanded its programs. It organized agricultural training programs, set up a Youth Aliyah that eventually brought nearly 3,500 young German Jews to Palestine, and stepped up illegal settlement in Palestine.

Eventually, some 80,000 Berlin Jews would emigrate between 1933 and 1939.

Why not more? Several factors discourgaged emigration. Many Jews believed that power would moderate the Nazi movement, or that the party's popularity would soon slacken. They looked back on earlier episodes of anti-Semitism—such as the Berlin Movement of the 1880s—that had flamed and quickly died. Some even clung to a "my country right or wrong" attitude, a belief that they could prove the Nazis wrong by showing how loyal they were even in times of hardship.

Many did not have the energy or desire to leave their homeland, to learn a new language or a new skill, or separate from family.

Other factors were beyond their control. Most countries were reluctant to accept Jewish immigrants. Visas were extremely hard to obtain and the application process long, complicated and expensive. For those without practical or transferable skills or relatives abroad able to vouch for them, the outlook was especially grim. In addition, the Nazi government stripped emigrants of their assets, meaning that those who left would be immediately impoverished.

Internal Emigration
A popular alternative for those remaining was a kind of "internal emigration." As Jews were increasingly excluded from the public sphere, they created compensating space among their co-religionists, partly from choice, partly out of necessity. In the face of per-

secution and defamation there grew a renewed interest in things Jewish. A sense of identification, initially forced upon them, grew to a be a point of pride.

Synagogue attendance boomed—one rabbi said that the doors had to be closed an hour before the beginning of services—as congregants sought solace and a safe haven. The inside of a synagogue was one of the few places where criticism of the government, even if oblique, could be heard: the meaning behind a sermon about the persecutions of Pharoah, for instance, or the fate of Haman, would be easily understood. At the same time, however, support for religious activities from the beleaguered Jewish Community decreased. The Community earlier sustained 40 synagogues and 43 rabbis; by the end of 1933, it could manage only 19 synagogues and 22 rabbis.

Self-Help

Out-of-work actors, musicians and other artists established the *Kulturbund deutscher Juden* (Cultural Union of German Jews) in June, 1933. This self-help group produced plays, operas, concerts, lectures and even established its own music label, Lukraphon, giving employment to artists while providing entertainment for a Jewish audience excluded from general cultural activities. The first theatrical performance in Berlin was, pointedly, Lessing's plea for tolerance, *Nathan the Wise*.

This pattern of self-help in the face of exclusion, choices born of necessity, extended to other spheres as well. Harrassment and Nazi indoctrination in the public schools caused many parents to send their children to the Community's religious schools or one of the several private Jewish schools that had recently opened. In addition to the standard curriculum

November 14:
The First Supplementary Decree of the Reich Citizenship Law for the first time legally defines a Jew. Its complicated definition is forced to fall back on religious, rather than "racial," criteria.

1936

April:
Jewish journalists are forbidden to practice their profession.

April 2:
Jewish children are expelled from public day-care centers.

July:
Jewish art dealers must close their shops.

1937

April 15:
Jews can no longer receive doctorates.

November 4:
Jews are forbidden to give the "German greeting" (Heil Hitler!).

1938

January 1:
Jews can no longer be members of the Red Cross.

July 25:
Jewish physicians lose their licenses.

August 17:
Jews are required to add "Israel" or "Sara" to their names.

and Jewish religious studies, these schools stressed foreign language instruction in order to facilitate emigration.

The Kristallnacht Pogrom

In 1938, after two years of relative calm—during which no major anti-Semitic legislation was introduced and some Jews hoped for a stabilization of the situation—the passion for persecution erupted again. Jews were forced to add "Israel" or "Sara" to their names. Their passports were stamped with a large red "J." Jewish veterans of World War I, previously exempt from many anti-Jewish measures, lost their special status. The Nazis took away the legal standing of Jewish public associations, thus abolishing, after 250 years of existence, the Jewish Community organization.

Still, this was only a prelude. During the night of November 9–10, 1938, there occurred the most extensive pogrom in Germany since the First Crusade 800 years earlier, a state-sponsored explosion of violence and destruction. The Kristallnacht pogrom shattered the remnant of remaining Jews and marked the first sure step toward extermination. The vicious night destroyed over 260 synagogues and approximately 7,500 shops in Germany and resulted in somewhere around 26,000 arrests and 90 deaths.

The spark of the pogrom is often said to be the assassination on November 7, 1938, of a minor official in the German embassy in Paris by a young Jew, Herschel Grynszpan. Its roots had more to do, however, with appeasing radical elements in the party unhappy with the "moderation" of the previous two years.

Berlin, as the capital city, was especially hard hit. Thousands of Jewish-owned shops were attacked and looted and broken glass littered those streets—Kurfürstendamm, Tauentzienstrasse, Wilmersdorfer Strasse, and the humbler commercial roads of the Scheunenviertel —with concentrations of Jewish-owned stores. Königstrasse (today Rathausstrasse), in the center of town, was so full of shattered glass that passersby were forced to walk in the middle of the street.

The magnificent synagogue on Fasanenstrasse, a landmark known throughout the country, was completely gutted. A group of SA members spread gasoline over the pews in the sanctuary and set them ablaze. Crowds gathered as the flames spread through the synagogue. The fire department watched the structure burn, under orders to step in only if the blaze spread to neighboring buildings.

The same fate befell, among others, the landmark synagogues on Prinzregentenstrasse, Lindenstrasse, and Fraenkelufer. Some houses of worship, such as those on Pestalozzistrasse and Rykestrasse, and the city's oldest synagogue on Heidereutergasse, were deemed too close to other buildings and were spared from the flames, though they did not escape looting and desecration. The Oranienburger Strasse synagogue, set alight, was saved from extensive damage by the local police precinct captain, Wilhelm Krützfeld, who, citing the building's landmark status, drove off an SA gang of arsonists at the point of a pistol.

In Berlin alone over 10,000 Jews were arrested and a collective fine of one billion Reichsmarks was levied on the Jewish population.

The Vise Tightens

The Kristallnacht pogrom was a turning point. It made it clear that Jewish life in Germany—even a severely circumscribed one—was not possible. Immediately following the night of terror, the city's synagogues were closed (a few were later allowed to reopen), Jewish children were expelled from state schools, Jewish newspapers were banned. A November 12 "Decree to Exclude Jews from German Economic Life" prohibited Jews from running a retail business or independent trade, thus clearing the way for a new wave of "Aryanizations," the forced sale of Jewish businesses. In Berlin, some one third of the 3,700 remaining Jewish-owned retail businesses were "Aryanized" and the rest simply shut down.

The central Jewish administrative body, the *Reichsvertretung*, was forced to close, to be replaced by a government-controlled organization called the *Reichsvereinigung*

September 27:
Jewish lawyers lose their right to practice.

October 5:
Passports held by Jews must be stamped with a "J."

November 15:
Jewish children are expelled from state schools.

December 3:
Jews are forbidden to go to movies, the theater, cabarets, concerts, museums, stadiums, and sports fields.

December 3:
The driving licenses of Jews are declared invalid.

December 8:
Jews are excluded from universities.

1939

January 17:
Jews can no longer work as dentists, dental technicians, or pharmacists.

February 21:
Jews must surrender all items of gold, silver, platinum and precious stones.

April 1:
Jews are no longer allowed to use public libraries.

April 30:
Jews can be thrown out of their apartments without reason or warning. Jews can rent apartments only from other Jews.

(National Association). This group, though composed basically of the same people, and still headed by Rabbi Baeck, was now essentially a part of the government bureaucracy, an agency to carry out Nazi directives pertaining to the Jews. Thus the *Reichsvereinigung* abetted Nazi repression—for example, compiling lists from their own files of people to be deported—and lent an aura of legitimacy to such Nazi outrages.

The behavior of the *Reichsvereinigung* remains controversial to this day. Many feel they were far too pliant, and that a principled stand of non-cooperation would have saved lives. Recent research however, paints a more complex picture of give and take and has also uncovered instances of resistance. One of them, a protest against the October 1940 deportation of Jews from provinces in southwest Germany, cost one member of the executive council, Julius Seligsohn, his life.

The Search for an Exit

There were about 80,000 Jews still living in the capital city on the night of the Kristallnacht pogrom, and they now engaged in a panicked search for an exit. As Rabbi Max Nussbaum recalled, "The struggle for a visa to a foreign country, any country, regardless what kind or how far away it was ('how far from what?' we used to ask as a joke), became the main preoccupation of every single Jew and of our Jewish organizations." Embassies were swamped by requests, huge lines formed outside the American Consulate and the Palestine Office, but the required visas and affidavits and certificates remained scarce. The number of entrants allowed into Palestine by the British government actually dropped. By the summer of 1940, the United States too had choked off entry.

Despite these barriers, there was a swell of emigration. In the first two months of 1939 alone, some 6,400 Berlin Jews left the country, more than the total for all of 1934. In the first nine months of the year, some 16,000 Jews left the city. These refugees found themselves headed for Central and South America, the Low Countries, even Shanghai, the only destination that did not require a visa.

Life During Wartime

The German invasion of Poland on September 1, 1939 inaugurated the deadliest war in history. Within a year Germany had conquered

Poland, France, Denmark, Norway, and the Low Countries and pushed the British forces off the continent. National Socialism, and its ideology of totalitarianism, militarism, and anti-Semitism, appeared invincible.

The war, far from distracting the government from its persecutions of Jews, prodded the Nazis to intensify them. Radios and telephones were prohibited, curfews instituted, certain quarters of the city declared off-limits, forced relocations to specially designated "Jewish houses" carried out. On September 1, 1941, a law revived the medieval practice of forcing Jews to wear a yellow badge.

Even before the war, Jews, after being expelled from their jobs, were subject to forced work on public labor projects. With the outbreak of hostilities, Jews were impressed into forced labor to serve Germany's war needs. Eventually over 25,000 Jews were doing forced labor in Berlin, many of them at large corporations such as Siemens, AEG and IG Farben, generally for about 72 Pfennigs an hour.

Eichmann in Berlin

In December 1939, Adolph Eichmann was appointed head of the Gestapo's "Jewish Affairs" department and set up shop in the former offices of the B'nai B'rith on Kurfürstenstrasse. A member of the SS since 1932, Eichmann had developed a reputation in the security service as an expert on the "Jewish Question" and had distinguished himself by organizing the removal of the Jewish population of Vienna. He was charged with performing the same feat in the capital of the Third Reich.

His first action was to establish a Central Office for Emigration in order to facilitate the flight of Jews from the capital. Although he

September:
It is forbidden to erect a sukkah in a synagogue courtyard; private persons are also prohibited from building a sukkah.

September 3:
Jews may not leave their apartments after 8pm (9pm in summer).

September 23:
Jews must surrender their radios.

1940

March 22:
The Jewish cemetery in Spandau is closed and dug up.

July 4:
Grocery shopping for Jews is restricted to the hour between 4pm and 5pm.

August:
Jews must surrender their telephones.

1941

September 1:
All Jews from the age of six are required to wear a yellow star in public.

October 10:
Jews are forbidden to leave their homes without police permission.

October 18:
Deportations of Jews from Berlin begin.

October 23:
Jews are no longer allowed to leave the country.

succeeded in simplifying the bureaucratic process from the German side, his scheme failed, since other countries were unwilling to accept great numbers of Jews.

At the same time that this failure became apparent, the German government faced another "setback": rather than losing Jews, the Third Reich was, due to its conquests in the east, actually gaining millions more.

The Final Solution

It was therefore decided, not later than the summer of 1941, that the "solution" to the "Jewish Problem" would have to be more radical and more sweeping; it would have to be a "final solution." Hitler had probably envisioned the physical destruction of Jewry from the very beginning of his political career, but it was only at this time, emboldened by his success and at the peak of his popularity, having the means and the territory and the followers at his disposal, that he could carry it out.

By the time of the Wannsee Conference, held on January 20, 1942 in a villa just outside Berlin, the extermination of Jews was already in progress in the east. The conference, chaired by the Chief of Security Police and Security Service Reinhard Heydrich, and with Eichmann in attendance, was called in order to iron out details and coordinate the massive effort within the Nazi bureaucracy. The deportation of Berlin's Jews had actually commenced some three months previously.

The Trains Roll East

On October 1, 1941—Yom Kippur—Rabbi Baeck, while in the middle of a sermon at Joachimstaler Synagogue, was ordered to a Gestapo meeting. He was told that the *Reichsvereinigung* was to prepare for the deportation of some Berlin Jews to work camps in the east. They were to compile lists, send out notifications, arrange for the orderly processing of the human cargo.

Baeck and the other Jewish leaders discussed whether they should carry out these orders and came to the conclusion that, the deportations being inevitable, it would be more humane if they handled the process rather than the Gestapo. They had no idea at that time, of course, that the destination was anywhere other than a labor camp. Still, as one *Reichsvereinigung* employee later remarked, the "relaxed, stoical quiescence with which the highest administrative body of Jewish autonomy allowed the National Socialist leaders to bring it into the deportation machinery appears to be astonishing."

The Levetzowstrasse Synagogue, which had survived the Kristallnacht pogrom without major damage, was turned into a collection point and processing center. One thousand Jews were told to report there with no more than one suitcase and one rucksack. From the former synagogue they were marched through the streets to the Putlitzbrücke freight depot in the Moabit district of Berlin. The first train, containing 1,013 Jews, departed for the Lodz ghetto in Poland on October 18, 1941.

The procedure of collecting and processing, eviction and entraining, the bureaucratic efficiency and brutal compulsion, continued, with variations, for the next three and a half years. The former Jewish Old Age Home on Grosser Hamburger Strasse superseded the Levetzowstrasse Synagogue as an assembly point. The Anhalter and Grunewald train stations joined the Putlitzbrücke station as departure points. The orderly issuing of deportation notices was replaced by arrests and incarceration prior to expulsion.

In all, 187 trains took some 55,000 Berlin Jews over the next three and a half years to the ghettos of Lodz, Riga, and Warsaw, among others, and the concentration camps at Sobibor, Sachsenhausen, Ravensbrück, Auschwitz and Theresienstadt. About 90–95% of these deportees died.

Berlin without Jews?

On June 16, 1943, the capital of the Third Reich was officially declared *judenrein*—"purified" of Jews.

But in fact there were several thousand

December 26:
Jews are forbidden to use public telephones.

1942

January 10:
Jews must surrender all furs and woolen materials, skis, ski boots and hiking boots.

February 17:
Jews can no longer buy newspapers or magazines.

March 26:
Jews must mark their apartments with a yellow star.

May 15:
Jews are forbidden to keep pets.

June 12:
Jews must surrender their electrical appliances, optical equipment, cameras, vacuum cleaners, bicycles, typewriters and record players.

June 30:
All Jewish educational institutions are shut down.

July 7:
Jews are forbidden to use public transportation.

September 18:
Jews no longer receive ration cards for meat, clothing, milk, tobacco, and white bread, among other items.

October 9:
Jews are no longer permitted to buy books.

Jews still in Berlin. Most of these were so-called privileged Jews, those married to non-Jewish spouses, who enjoyed a special status and were exempt from many of the persecutions visited upon their co-religionists. There were also several thousand Jews living in the capital illegally and secretly: "U-boats," they were called, German for submarine.

Survival and Resistance

Most of these Jews went underground in late 1942 or early '43 as rumors began circulating about the fate of the Jews shipped east. Some assumed new identities and lived and worked as "Aryans"; others remained hidden, often for years, rarely, if ever, daring to venture out; most were constantly on the move, constantly in fear.

Others adopted a more active resistance. The Herbert Baum Group, a network of young Jewish communists, engaged in propaganda and sabotage until they were arrested and executed after an arson attack on a Nazi exhibit in June 1942. Other groups engaging in resistance in Berlin included the (not exclusively Jewish) *Gemeinschaft für Frieden und Aufbau* (Community for Peace and Reconstruction) and *Chug Chaluzi* (Pioneer Circle), a group of young Zionists.

The Fall of the Third Reich

Even as the Soviets began their great push from Stalingrad to Berlin and the tide of war turned against the German army, the trains continued to roll. The last deportation, bound for Theresienstadt, left Berlin on March 27, 1945, after the American army had crossed the Rhine River in the west and as the Soviet Army prepared to sweep over the Oder River in the east, long after it was certain the Germans would go down to defeat. Three weeks later, on April 29, Hitler, in his underground bunker near Potsdamer Platz, wrote his last "political testament" blaming the war on Jewry. He then committed suicide. On May 8, 1945, Germany surrendered unconditionally.

In the still-smoking rubble of Berlin, some 7,000 Jews emerged into the light: about 1,300 had survived in hiding, some 1,500 had just returned from concentration camps, and 4,200 had survived as "privileged Jews." On May 11, just three days after the death of the monstrous Third Reich, Jews in Berlin held their first service in a building in the Weisensee Jewish Cemetery, a congregation of free people once more.

Reestablishment: The Post-War Community

At the end of the war Berlin was a heap of ruins. Almost one-fifth of its buildings had been destroyed or heavily damaged, almost one-third of its apartments were uninhabitable. Thirty percent of the city's streets were destroyed. The historic and imposing palaces, theaters and civic buildings along Unter den Linden, Wilhelm-strasse, Potsdamer Platz and elsewhere in the city center lay in ruins. The German population too, Führer-less and utterly defeated, was broken.

Following agreements among the victorious Allies, Germany was divided into three (and after France was included, four) different zones: The British and American zones were in the north-west and south-west of Germany, the French received a portion in the west, and the Russians were in charge of the east of the country. Although deep within the Soviet sector of the country, Berlin was also divided into four separate parts.

The Superpower Chill

Relations between the Western powers and the Soviet Union, however, quickly chilled into the tension and antagonism of Cold War. This confrontation made cooperation among the sectors impossible, and in 1949, two separate German states emerged: the Soviet sector became the communist German Democratic Republic (East Germany) and the three Allied sectors were transformed into the Federal Republic of Germany (West Germany).

Berlin, deep within the new communist state, remained divided, with three-fourths of the city under the administration of the Allies (and later the Federal Republic of Germany) but far away from West Germany. It would remain so, locked in a condition popularly referred to as the "stabilization of the impossible," for the next half century. Berlin was turned into the frontline of the Cold War, a stage for major-power politics, and a city of spies, tension and intrigue.

The Cold War also meant a quick rehabilitation for West Germany and a glossing over of its Nazi past as the US marshalled the newly democratic state as an ally against communism. The overwhelming majority of participants in Nazi war crimes received no sentences or only token punishments. Many Nazis, in fact, attained high posts in the new government, the most prominent examples being Hans Globke, who provided commentary to the infamous Nazi Nuremberg Laws and after the war served as state secretary for West Germany's first chancellor Konrad Adenauer, and Kurt Kiesinger, a former Nazi Party member, who served as the country's chancellor from 1966 to '69.

Post-War Jewish Life

The Jewish communities of Germany had, in every respect, been laid totally to waste. For Jews, there was a complete break with the German-Jewish past and little thought of a future in Germany. The majority of the few thousand survivors were intent on leaving as soon as possible. "We cannot suppose," said Robert Weltsch, a former Berliner active before Hitler in the Zionist movement, "that there are Jews who feel attracted to Germany. Germany has the smell of dead bodies, gas and torture chambers. It is no soil for Jews."

Ironically, though, at this very moment, Berlin, like the rest of Germany, experienced a huge influx of Jews. Between 1945 and 1950 some 200,000 refugees, mainly Yiddish-speaking, often observant, Jews of East European origin, fled west to Allied-controlled Germany. Known as Displaced Persons, DPs for short, these Jews, without homes or families and facing new waves of anti-Semitism in their native lands, sought a safe haven, usually in Palestine (or after 1948, Israel) or the United States. They found themselves laid up in Germany to be processed and to wait for visas, work permission and passage.

During this ordeal, which could last from 48 hours to several years, they were housed in camps organized by the American army and the United Nations Relief and Rehabilitation Administration. In Berlin there were five DP camps, some occupying former US military barracks and one in a former Nazi barracks.

For a few years the camps were centers of Jewish life, where schools, theater groups, synagogues and Yiddish-language newspapers flourished. But emigration remained the primary goal, and, seven years after the end of the war, when the last of the DPs were finally able to leave the "accursed land," as they called Germany, the camps were closed.

Yet some Jews, both DPs and pre-war residents, stayed in Berlin. The reasons were as varied as human nature: personal ties, business, sickness, lethargy, procrastination.

The Jews that Remained

A new Jewish Community organization first appeared in the middle of May, 1945, and was recognized as a legal body in February, 1946. The executive council was made up principally of German Jews who had survived the concentration camps; only one, Hans-Erich Fabian, was active in the pre-war Community leadership. By the end of 1945 there were some 7,000 members.

This organization was dubbed a "liquidation community"—a temporary agency established to tie up a few loose ends before dissolving itself. It was intended to ensure that, while members prepared to emigrate, some social and religious services were provided and to aid in the search for family members and the filing of reparation claims. The three synagogues that had survived Nazi desecration and war-time bombing—those on Rykestrasse, Pestalozzistrasse and the small weekday synagogue on Fraenkelufer—were repaired, renovated and rededicated. A kindergarten was established. A newspaper, which among news and opinion articles also featured "missing persons" classified ads, began publication.

Isolation and Obligation

The reconstruction of Jewish life in Berlin was an ambivalent undertaking. In the first years the Jews of Germany encountered almost total isolation from Jews and Jewish organizations in the rest of the world who felt it was shameful and traitorous to live in the land of the murderers.

Yet others felt that the presence of Jews in Germany marked an important victory over Naziism and anti-Semitism. With no Jews in the country, they argued, Hitler would have won. As Hans Frey, the editor of a postwar German-Jewish newspaper put it, "We German Jews have not only the right, but the obligation, to stay in Germany and to rebuild what was taken from us."

The Character of the Community

Of course, what could be rebuilt was only a faint echo of the influential and robust pre-Third Reich Jewish Berlin. The character of the Community had undergone fundamental changes, the most notable of which was that it was no longer, for the most part, German. Only about ten percent of the postwar community had German roots; the majority was Polish, Hungarian, and Czechoslovakian.

The venerable pre-war split between Reform and Orthodox segments did not survive the war. Because many members of the new communities were from more devout eastern European backgrounds, and because it was felt to be important, as a sign of survival and solidarity, to define their organization as a rigorous and "authentic" one, the new community adopted only traditional rites. In the land of its birth, Reform Judaism existed no more.

The Rise of Galinski

In January 1948 the first election for the executive committee of the Jewish Community organization took place (the prior administration had been appointed). Among the representatives elected was Heinz Galinski, who was to play a pivotal role in the development of Jewish life in Berlin and throughout Germany. The next year he became president of the Berlin Community, a position he was to maintain for the next 44 years until his death in 1992.

Galinski was born in Marienburg in northern Germany in 1912. He survived Auschwitz, Buchenwald and Bergen-Belsen, and returned to Berlin, his pre-war home, after his liberation in April, 1945. He was an early proponent of reestablishing Jewish life in Germany, although he was a staunch Zionist and fought against any reform and assimilationist tendencies within the Community.

His political clout was far more powerful than the electoral strength of his constituency (which was practically nil) and he had a profound effect on the course of Jewish life in Berlin. He influenced, for example, some of the first laws for prosecuting former Nazis and negotiated agreements that brought Russian Jews to Berlin after 1989, a development that has lately changed the face of Jewish Berlin.

Galinski was not without his critics, however. He had a reputation as an autocratic and domineering leader, reluctant to compromise or delegate authority.

Berlin Divided

In 1952, Stalin instituted an anti-Jewish campaign that resulted, in all the Soviet satellite countries, in anti-Semitic persecutions. The Jews in East Germany, too, came under suspicion, accused of being agents of Zionism and American imperialism, and many were purged from positions of power in the state and party bureaucracies.

When Julius Meyer, head of the Jewish communities in East Germany, fled to West Berlin, the crisis came to a head. For a time all Jewish institutions in East Germany were closed down. The rabbi of Berlin, Nathan Levinson, recommended that all Jews in East Germany resettle in the West. In January 1953, the Berlin Jewish Community split into separate organizations, one serving those in the west, another for those residing in the east.

With Stalin's death in 1953 the crisis ended and Jewish life in East Germany— an undemonstrative and reserved one—resumed. With a government that was atheist and anti-Zionist, Jewish practice was extremely difficult. The number of Community members in East Berlin dwindled from about 1,500 just after the war to about 200 by the early 1980s. A single shul, the large Rykestrasse Synagogue, was more than adequate for the few worshippers.

The character of the community in the east was quite different than that of the west. Those in the communist German Democratic Republic were predominantly assimilated German Jews who had returned to their homeland in order to build a new socialist and anti-fascist society. Most of them did not define themselves as Jews in a religious or nationalistic way, nor did they become members of the Jewish communities. Prominent examples include writers Anna Seghers, Stefan Heym and Arnold Zweig, and composers Hanns Eisler and Paul Dessau.

In contrast, the Jews of West Berlin were more religiously and less politically oriented. Membership of the Community hovered at around 7,000, a figure that remained stable until the late 1980s. Emigration and a high death rate among the aged population was balanced by immigration from those fleeing anti-Semitism in eastern Europe, particularly from Hungary in 1956 and Poland in 1968.

On a Permanent Footing

By the late 1950s, it was clear that the Berlin Jewish Community was a permanent one. In 1959, on the site of the destroyed synagogue on Fasanestrassse, a new Jewish Community Center was dedicated, a conscious statement that the Community was here to stay.

The next two decades were years of consolidation and expansion. An adult education program was initiated in 1962. In 1969, religious instruction for Jewish students was introduced in five city schools. A new kindergarten, the first new Jewish school building in Germany since the Holocaust, was built in 1971. An old age home was erected in 1978.

For these and other projects, the tiny Community was dependent upon subsidies from the government. This support came from the Germans partly in a spirit of moral obligation. But it was also felt, both within and without the country, that the fledgling German democracy would be judged by the treatment of its Jews. The German government was therefore eager to provide well for the Jews on its soil as part of the price for readmission to the community of nations.

The Packed Suitcase Syndrome

But though the organizational life of Berlin's Jews became stronger and more permanently established, inner life was still underdeveloped. What became known as the "packed suitcase syndrome" was prevelant: the feeling that one was ready to leave at anytime, that life in Berlin was impermanent. The community was insular and self-conscious. There was a lack of grass-roots organizations among Jews and a lack of a public presence in the greater society.

Part of this recalcitrance was undoubtedly due to the attitudes of German society at large, where, for two decades after the war, a wall of silence surrounded the years of terror. The *Wirtschaftswunder*, the economic miracle of the 1950s, when the German economy boomed with the aid of Marshall Plan money, diverted the public's attention to material concerns. As a best-selling book later phrased it, there was "an inability to mourn."

The taboo was finally shattered in the late '60s by the youth movement, which for the first time confronted the older generation with questions and accusations about the past. But this public discussion did not really become focused on the Jewish experience during the Third Reich until 1979, when the American TV series "Holocaust," adapted from the Gerald Green novel of the same name, was shown on West German television, attracting some 12 million viewers. Along with a stormy debate over the value of this fictionalized account of a German-Jewish family came a flurry of attention on the fate of Jews in the Third Reich, Jewish history, and Jewish culture.

The Suitcases are Unpacked

Not coincidentally, given the more sympathetic mood in the larger society, Jewish life in Berlin in the 1980s, both West and East, envinced a new dynamism. One of the earliest manifestations of this in West Berlin was the appearance in 1982 of the *Jüdische Gruppe Berlin* (Berlin Jewish Group), formed to protest the Israeli invasion of Lebanon. This was one of the first Jewish activist, grass-roots groups to spring up in post-war Berlin, and also one of the first to go public with its opposition to Community policy.

Protests against the visit of Ronald Reagan to the SS military cemetery in Bitburg in May, 1985, and outrage over a play, "Garbage, the City and Death," in Frankfurt (considered by many to be anti-Semitic), also helped to foment a new high-profile public stance. For the first time large groups of West German Jews were raising their voices in front of the German public and media, no longer willing to keep their anger and concerns within the small, closed circle of their co-religionists.

In East Berlin, too, a new public stance was developing. This had something to do with a change in policy of the communist government, which, as part of an attempt to build trade ties with the United States, began to encourage Jewish activities. The government provided money for the reconstruction of the New Synagogue on Oranienburgerstrasse and supported other Jewish cultural events, in particular those marking the 50th anniversary of the Kristallnacht pogrom on November 9, 1988.

Responding to these changes, as well as to the new climate of "perestroika" in the socialist state, a group of secular Jews informally organized a group called *Wir für Uns* (We for Ourselves) in order to celebrate holidays and to study and enjoy their long-neglected religious inheritance. This group later evolved into the *Jüdischer Kulturverein* (The Jewish Culture Society), which, though now well-established, maintains its dissident style.

It was around this time too, that the independent orthodox congregation Adass Yisroel, founded in 1869 and destroyed by the Nazis, was reestablished in East Berlin. Mario Offenberg, the son of a former member, successfully petitioned the newly receptive East German administration, which allowed the reorganization of the congregation and the return of some of its pre-war property.

The Wall Falls

On November 9, 1989, the anniversary of the Kristallnacht pogrom, the Berlin Wall was opened, and shortly afterwards the German Democratic Republic collapsed. In October 1991, Germany was reunited, the former communist territory folded into the Federal Republic of Germany.

Reunification changed the political landscape of Germany in many ways, some of them troubling. An aggressive and violent right-wing extremism emerged, the result of a renewed national chauvinism and economic collapse in the east. Several shocking incidents in the years following reunification—firebombings in the cities of Mölln and Solingen that killed several Turkish children, two separate arson attacks on the small synagogue in Lübbeck—seemed to confirm fears of a new wave of German racism, anti-Semitism and hate.

Nationally, this wave seemed to reach a high point in the mid 1990s: in '93 some 656 anti-Semitic incidents were reported nationwide, 72 of them violent; in '94 1,366 incidents, 41 of them violent. Public outrage and protest and more stringent legal efforts seemed to have improved the situation since then. In 1995, the government reported 958 anti-Semitic incidents; in 1996, 719.

Berlin, a liberal stronghold, remained relatively free of such actions. According to official statistics, Berlin experienced 112 anti-Semitic incidents in 1995 and 84 in 1996. Very few of these were assaults against persons; they were mainly arson attacks, vandalism, hate mail and bomb threats. Several monuments and memorials have been wrecked or graffitied over the last several years, and the Schönhauser Allee and Weissensee cemeteries are not infrequently desecrated.

Jewish Reunification

The reunification of the city also reunited the city's two Jewish Community organizations. Of even greater significance to Jewish Berlin, however, has been the arrival in the city since the late 1980s of some 12,000–16,000 Jews from the former Soviet Union. In 1991, with the prodding of Community leader Heinz Galinski, the West German government assigned a special quota and refugee status to Jews from the former Soviet Union. Since then over 50,000 have come to Germany, making it the third most popular destination, after Israel and the United States, for Jews from the former Soviet Union.

Their presence has had a striking effect throughout Germany. In Berlin the size of the Jewish Community has almost doubled to about 11,000 due to this influx. New institutions and clubs—the Jüdische Galerie, which features the works of artists from the former Soviet Union, and a club for Red Army veterans, among others—have been created. Many events are now carried out in Russian. The adult education program offers several courses of religious instruction in Russian. Since early 1997, all the material in the Community magazine has appeared in both German and Russian.

Still, the integration has not been seamless. Many of those from the former Soviet Union accuse the Community organization of high-handedness and arrogance. Others complain of not feeling at home in an organization dominated by German-speakers. For some, the Jewish Culture Society, with its east German roots and many Russian-speakers, provides a more comfortable alternative.

The New Face of Jewish Berlin

The Jewish Community currently boasts some 11,000 members. The structures to support this group are extensive. The Community administers six synagogues; two old-age homes; a nursing home; a mikveh; a kindergarten; an elementary school; a high school; a gymnasium; a youth center; a library; an adult education program; an art gallery; three cemeteries; and a wide array of groups and activities, from B'nai B'rith to the Zionist Organization of Germany. It is the largest Jewish Community in Germany.

And the Jewish Community is no longer the only game in town. The independent Adass Yisroel congregation claims 300 members and maintains a synagogue; an educational program; a kosher café; a kosher grocery store; and a cemetery. The Jewish Culture Society, with some 300 members, offers a rich program of religious and cultural activities. The Centrum Judaicum Foundation, which administers the exhibitions, events, and archive at the New Synagogue, is an important presence. Several national organizations, such as the Central Council of Jews in Germany, have recently relocated to the new capital.

A clutch of restaurants, cafés and retail stores have opened, many in former east Berlin, and while they cannot really be called centers of Jewish life—the customers are more often than not non-Jews—these establishments show a willingness to manifest a public presence that was long absent here.

There is new vigor and variety too, in the religious life of Jewish Berlin. Reform-style services have recently been reintroduced. An independent group meets monthly for shabbat services with a feminist orientation. The Jewish Culture Society holds an informal

Kabbalat Shabbat services every week and lively celebrations of the festivals.

The city's Orthodox wing has been active as well. In 1996, a Chabad Lubavitch center opened. The resident rabbi and his wife conduct an energetic program of classes, study groups, personal instruction, and special events with an emphasis on students and Russian Jews. Two new programs sponsored by the Central Welfare Office of Jews in Germany, Ken HaMisrach and Eshet Chail, provide regular programs on law and traditions. The Adass Yisroel congregation offers a home as well for devout Berliners.

In addition, there are a dozen or so independent groups—religious, cultural, and political—that have bolstered Jewish life in the city. Many of these groups, such as the left-wing *Jüdische Gruppe Berlin* or the gay and lesbian group *Yachad,* provide a place for Jews who are otherwise uncomfortable within the Community.

That organization too is responding to new times. In elections in June, 1997, members of the Jewish Community elected their first leader from the post-Holocaust generation, Andreas Nachama (the son of the Community's popular cantor). He and the new board of directors are shaking off some of the dust that had settled around the previous administration. They have eased some of the old antagonism to independent groups such as the Jewish Culture Society and the Adass Yisroel congregation. There's a new willingness to recognize and respond to the considerable reformist bloc within the Community. And the organization is attempting to better serve Russian-speaking Jews with, among other initiatives, a new "Integration Bureau." There is, all in all, a refreshing openness and enthusiasm.

The Challenges Ahead

There remain great challenges for Nachama and the new board of directors. The Community's political clout has diminished in the last decade, even as its numbers rise. This decline is due in part to the loss of the politically savvy Galinski, and in part to the fading, after 50 years, of the exceptional consideration once given to the Jews of Germany. At the same time, the city of Berlin, strapped for cash, has threatened the funding of several Jewish Community projects, almost all of which continue to depend heavily on government subsidies.

In addition, there are the problems that the Jews of Berlin share with Jewish communities around the world: differences among congregants over religious practices, fears about keeping young people within the fold, debates about directions for the future.

Yet Jewish life in Germany is different than that in other communities. The shadow of history is inescapable, giving rise to other and perhaps more profound questions. What is the proper response to the German past? Is there a future for Jews in Berlin? Is it possible for Jews to live a "normal" Jewish life here?

These questions have no definitive answers. Without resolving them or ignoring them, Jews in the German capital continue to worship and celebrate, and now in greater numbers and with greater vitality than at any time since the war.

Index